I0575804

FOUR OLD ICELANDIC SAGAS AND OTHER TALES

Translated by

W. Bryant Bachman, Jr.

The University of Southwestern Louisiana

UNIVERSITY PRESS OF AMERICA

LANHAM • NEW YORK • LONDON

University Press of America,® Inc.

4720 Boston Way
Lanham, MD 20706

3 Henrietta Street
London WC2E 8LU England

Printed in the United States of America

Library of Congress Cataloging in Publication Data
Main entry under title:

Four old Icelandic sagas and other tales.

Bibliography: p.
Contents: The saga of Clever Ref — The story of Thorstein of the East Fjords — The saga of Valla Ljot — [etc.]
1. Sagas. 2. Old Norse literature—Translations into English. 3. English literature—Translations from Old Norse. I. Bachman, W. Bryant, 1941-
PT7262.E5F6 1985 839'.63 85-7394
ISBN 0-8191-4703-6
ISBN 0-8191-4704-4 (pbk.)

ISBN 13 978-0-8191-4704-2

To my students

ACKNOWLEDGMENTS

The debt I owe to preceding scholarship is large, and I am perhaps most indebted to the fine editions of the *Íslenzk fornrit* series from which this translation was made. I should also like to acknowledge the helpful suggestions concerning *Valla-Ljóts saga* made by Alan Berger, of Cornell University, and the general encouragement and support throughout the course of this project afforded by Jess B. Bessinger, Jr. of New York University, by James M. Dunn, formerly of Princeton University, and by Duncan Carter, of Boston University. The errors and other infelicities that remain in this work are, of course, my own.

TABLE OF CONTENTS

PREFACE

This collection was intended first to bring English readers several Old Icelandic works of genuine literary merit, and second, to include in these works some of the more humorous material written about the Saga Age, in particular, *Króka Refs saga*, *Sneglu-Halli þáttr*, and the *Bandamanna saga*. To the best of my knowledge none of the works in this collection have published English translations, though there have been several English translations of the *Möðruvallabók* version of the *Bandamanna* saga, and Lee M. Hollander in his *The Skalds* (Univ. of Michigan: 1945) paraphrases parts of the shorter *Morkinskinna* version of *Sneglu-Halli þáttr* and translates the poetry of that version.

The poems found in the originals of most of these stories are written in an intricate and demanding meter which, combined with the generous use of elaborate kennings, tends to make literal translation of them incomprehensible. (Non-specialist readers can find general discussions of the skaldic art listed in the selected bibliography of this collection.) Thus, in the belief that retention of the original metrical, rhyme, and alliterative constraints produces on the modern English ear an effect very different from that envisioned by the skalds for their audiences, and in the interests of preserving as much of the original meaning of the poem as possible, I have chosen to recreate these poems quite idiomatically, without the original constraints, but preserving as many of the kennings as possible.

INTRODUCTION

Króka Refs saga:

Króka Refs saga (The Saga of Clever Ref) is one of the last Family Sagas, probably written fairly early in the fourteenth century. It is preserved wholly in only one vellum, AM 471, 4to, but fragments of it exist in two other vellums, Stockh. Perg. nr. 8, 4to, and AM 586, 4to. It survives also in several paper copies. This translation is made from the edition of Jóhannes Halldórsson in the Íslenzk fornrit series, vol. xiv, 1959, pp. 117-160. This edition is taken primarily from the vellums that are most closely related, AM 471, 4to, and Stockh. Perg. nr. 8, 4to.

The historicity of this saga is especially doubtful. Neither Landámabók nor any of the other sagas corroborate the existence of the Icelandic characters in Króka Refs saga. The one exception is Gest Oddleifson, said in this saga to be the maternal uncle of Ref. Gest has an independent existence in several major sagas. Furthermore, the internal chronology of the saga is defective. The story is initially set in Iceland sometime prior to 960 (the death of Norway's Hakon the Good). The locale of the story rapidly shifts to Greenland for a number of years, then finally to Norway during the reign of Harald Sigurdson (1046-66). That means a period of at least eighty-six years must have elapsed between Ref's adolescence and his arrival in Norway. Whatever this confusion may suggest about the sources used by the author, it tends to confirm that Króka Refs saga is more a product of imagination than of history. The story of Króka Ref is not told elsewhere in Icelandic literature, although there are some structural similarities between it and the well-known Auðunar þáttr Vestfirzka, and some minor resemblances to the Greenland episodes of Fóstbroeðra saga.

Among the characters of Icelandic sagas, Ref is fairly unique. His most salient characteristic is an abundance of native wit and skill, and the saga reemphasizes this at every turn in the narrative. This is not to say that clever characters are at all unusual in the sagas (one could quickly point out several such characters in just this collection of translations), but this type of characterization as a sustaining unity in a saga is rare. In *Króka Refs saga* almost every single incident seems designed to produce wonderment at the virtuosity, almost wizardry, of this character who with one strategem or another manages to elude his enemies for some twenty years. His repertoire is seemingly inexhaustible. From his domestic sprinkler system to his wheeled boat, his shipboard ruses to his disguises, Ref meets every situation with masterful skill. Only in his youth does Ref show little of these talents. There he seemed to be an idler of little promise, and a source of great vexation to his parents. But appearances are deceptive, and this same little boy who presumably so irritated his parents by taking apart a toy ship in front of the fire was later, single-handedly and without prior experience, to build flawlessly the greatest ship in the land. Interestingly, it was not until Gest Oddleifson expressed some confidence in him that Ref began to distinguish himself. In other sagas where he appears, Gest is usually presented as a man of special wisdom, of prescience almost, and his expression of confidence in Ref early in this saga surely bodes well for the future of this character. It is Gest who tells Ref that he must have a saga written about him, for he senses that Ref is "the smartest of all our kinsmen" (11).

As with the *Bandamanna saga*, another late work, the concerns of the blood feud are largely peripheral in *Króka Refs saga*. The saga is far more intently focused on the cleverness and humor of Ref's escapades. Though the blood feud does activate the saga at crucial points (Ref leaves Iceland to escape the avenging Gunnar), it does not precipitate the ever-widening circle of complication usually found in the older sagas. Indeed, it seems that its chief function in this saga is to generate sympathy for the protagonist. All of Ref's slayings are either in self-defense or in response to intolerable insult. Moreover, in the last instance, the insults of Gellir and the Thorgilsons, a considerable time elapses between the insults and Ref's revenge, a fact which tends to emphasize the forebearance as well as the judiciousness of the hero. He does not act until the situation becomes really intolerable, and until he is fully prepared for the consequences. Only once does Ref act without due consideration, in his immediate killing of Grani, but there this traditional heroic impetuousity is quickly subordinated by the author to the excitement of the skillful and witty announcement of the killing by means of puns. The older ethos of the classical sagas is largely absent from this saga. It has little of the flavor, for example, of *Valla-Ljóts saga*, a tale which centers on the concerns of the blood feud. If one could locate the ~~epicenter of~~ *Króka-Refs saga*, it would most likely be found in Ref's rejoinder to his future wife's foster brother, Thormod. "'A man should first have some plan in mind,' Ref said, 'before doing risky things'" (14).

Þórsteins þáttr Austfirðings:

Þórsteins þáttr Austfirðings (The Story of Thorstein of the East Fjords) is a very short story that exists only in independent form. It is not included in any collection of other material, as many of the shorter episodic narratives were. It is generally thought to be a late work, possibly as late as the fourteenth century. The story is preserved in two paper manuscripts, AM 562i, 4to, and AM 496, 4to. This translation is made from the edition of Jón Jóhannesson in *Íslenzk fornrit*, xi (1950), pp. 327-32.. The edition is based on AM 562i, a better text, though less directly derived from the original vellum than AM 496.

The story is set during the reign of Magnus the Good, and apparently the time of Magnus' attempts to subjugate Svein Ulfson (1042-47), though it is extremely doubtful that the story reflects any actual events. Thorstein is not known elsewhere in Icelandic literature or history. Most likely this tale was an Icelandic adaptation of an international folk tale of the type which now is usually called "The King in Disguise." The story also contains many structural and verbal similarities to the more well-known *Auðunar þáttr Vestfirzka*, and the author could well have been influenced by it.

Valla Ljóts saga:

Valla Ljóts saga (The Saga of Valla Ljot) is a classical Family Saga. It was written in the first half of the thirteenth century, probably during the period of 1220 to 1240. It survives in many paper manuscripts, all of which can be traced to one or the other of two versions of the saga represented by paper manuscripts AM 496 4to and AM 161, fol. Unfortunately, both of these have been very carelessly written and abound in errors. Furthermore, both also descend from a vellum which was, in all likelihood, very corrupt. The edition from which this translation is made is that of Jonas Kristiansson in *Íslenzk fornrit,* ix (1956), pp. 231-60. This edition is based on AM 161. Due to the textual problems with this saga, the translation often adopts variant readings when they seem preferable.

The events of this saga, insofar as any of them are historical, took place on the northern coast of Iceland probably shortly after the official acceptance of Christianity in the year 1000. Most of the main characters of the saga are attested elsewhere in Icelandic literature and historical documents, but the historicity of the events in the saga is problematic. In a related saga, *Svarfdoela saga*, there is a reference to Ljot's slaying of Halli.

In many ways the structure of this saga centers on Sigurd's deathbed advice to his sons in the opening scene. He tells them, "Don't be small--minded, but be careful of your honor" (43). What he seems to be asking them to do is to exercise careful judgment in walking the fine line between an overzealous pursuit of personal honor and a proper vigilance concerning it. Learn to distinguish between the trivial and the real, it might be paraphrased, and act accordingly. That this counsel is of prime concern in the saga can be seen from the fact that its disregard causes the death of two of the sons and the disgrace of the third. On the other hand, the hero of the saga, Valla Ljot, is a virtual exemplar of the counsel. Ljot combines a large measure of tolerance and forebearance with a very clear sense of where to draw the line.

Halli's behavior is perhaps the most blatant disregard of the old man's counsel. Even in the face of the consent of his mother and both his brothers to the proposed marriage to Torfi, Halli opposes the match, an eminently reasonable one and profitable to both sides, on the slender grounds that his mother's marriage to a freedman would not be honorable. With this predisposition, it is only too likely that in the ensuing scene, Halli finds Torfi's behavior insulting. There is a strong suggestion of naivety on Torfi's part in this scene. He is perfectly willing to give up the pig, but at the moment he himself is busy, and thus he thinks it is only sensible that Halli catch it himself. When Halli responds that such an act is beneath his dignity, Torfi answers with a kind of practical jocularity that indicates a benign tolerance for the arrogance of this youth (Halli at the time is seventeen years old). Halli chooses to ignore the offhand, jocular context of the remark, however, and applies it literally as justification for a homicide. Torfi, puzzled at the strange behavior of the youth, chooses to ignore Halli's charge and sends him away much in the manner any adult would caution a wayward child sent on an errand. He says only, "Now take it back and give it to your mother" (45). Halli's behavior at the pigpen foreshadows his behavior later in life. He remains contentious, quarrelsome, and arrogant throughout the saga. His own chieftain, Gudmund the Mighty, treats Halli well, but in return is only insulted by Halli when he implies that it is Gudmund's leadership that is causing the best men to leave Modruvale. Gudmund remains tolerant in this scene, however, and counsels Halli on the perils of his impending challenge of Valla Ljot. That Halli's challenge will not succeed is strongly suggested in the saga both by the highly stylized portrait of Ljot at the end of this scene and the remark about his relationship with the Svardalers, "among them, he alone ruled" (49). Halli's subsequent actions highlight Ljots' forebearqance as well as Halli's own arrogance. Ljot chooses to ignore the discourtesy of Halli's settling in the valley without permission. He acts with wisdom and forebearance in the matter of Halli's challenge of the land division. "I would rather pay the money," he says, "and get friendship in return" (50). It is only after Halli aggravated the challenge beyond all bounds (though the saga is not too clear on this, the merry-making of Halli at the Yule feast at Grund probably included malicious ridicule of Ljot in the matter of the land division), that Ljot settles on violence.

A settlement is made for Halli's death, though Gudmund is not too happy with it. Soon, Halli's brother, Hrolf, breaks that settlement and slays Ljot's nephew, Thorvard. Even though he was unhappy with the first settlement, this act of disobedience by one of his own Thingmen so angers Gudmund that he wants Ljot to be generously compensated this time, and he settles on Thorvard's death double the usual amount, noting in passing that, "those serve the district best who keep men from doing such harm" (55). Ljot's response is a model of forebearance. In accepting the settlement he makes the rather remarkable statement that, "he would rather be attacked again than offend anyone" (55).

The final slaying, that of the innocent Bodvar, is both prefaced and followed by an unusual emphasis on forebearance and the reluctance to kill. Bjorn has to be strongly goaded into the feud, even though it is his own brother that lies unavenged. Speaking of Bodvar, he admits, "The man is guiltless and has never been a part of the quarrels here in the land. It would be much more fitting if he were Hrolf; yet, even then it wouldn't be right" (58). The settlement is echoed by Ljot's response. He will have no part of it. He admonishes Bjorn, "Is this your plan, kinsman, to slay a guiltless man and break the peace? I'll not go on this journey" (59). He does not go, nor, clearly, does he approve of it, yet he also does not stop them. Apparently, somewhere in between lies the fine line seperating forebearance and a proper concern for honor. The aftermath of Bodvar's death is characterized by sorrow on the part of both Gudmund and Ljot for what has happened, yet the feud has now so escalated that they are both involved in it as principals. Gudmund goes after Ljot himself. But even now he exercises a measure of restraint, telling his men not to use weapons on Ljot. The issue is finally resolved at the Althing only through the willingness to compromise on the part of Ljot. He drops his case against Gudmund for the attack on his life, a case which the demands of personal honor argue strongly for. Gudmund is impressed by this, takes the opportunity to reduce the escalation of the feud and offers Ljot a sword. The exchange of the sword follows, and Ljot concludes, "you still hold your honor, and we can end our quarrel" (64). This backing off by Ljot from a rigid, unbending pursuit of personal honor is balanced in the closing pages of the saga by a similar sacrifice by Gudmund. He forces Hrolf, his own Thingman, to deliver up the money extorted from the fishermen, and the saga ends in complete reconciliation. Old Sigurd would have approved.

Þórvardar þáttr Krákunefs:

Þórvardar þáttr Krákunefs (The Story of Thorvard Crow-Nose) is a short narrative likely written very early in the thirteenth century. It is preserved both in *Morkinskinna* (Gl. kgl. saml. 1009, fol.) and in *Flateyjarbók* (Gl. kgl. saml. 1005, fol.). This translation is made from the edition of Guðni Jonsson in *Íslenzk fornrit*, vi (1943), pp. 369-74. The edition is based on the *Morkinskinna* text. Though this story is found in King Harald's saga in *Morkinskinna*, it does not present Harald in a very favorable light. In the old Germanic societies, it was customary not to refuse a gift, and once accepted, the gift must be repaid. The striking generousity of Eyestein Orri in this story exemplifies the latter part of this social dictum, and provides a strong contrast to Harald's ill-tempered refusal of the gift in the first part of the story. In fact, the story is at least as much about Eystein's magnamimous conduct as it is about Thorvard's generosity or Harald's ill-temper, though it is Thorvard for whom the story is named and it is Harald in whose saga the story is found.

Sneglu-Halla þáttr:

Sneglu-Halla þáttr (The Story of Shuttle-Halli) is an unusually long example of its genre, and it survives in two different versions. A considerably shortened version is found in *Morkinskinna* (Gl. kgl. saml. 1005, fol.) The longer version is found in *Flateyjarbók* (Gl. kgl. saml. 1005, fol.). The latter version appears more unified and was thus chosen for translation. Since the *Morkinskinna* version was probably cut at the time of its inclusion in *Morkinskinna*, the *Flateyjarbók* version may also be closer to the original source which, evidence suggests, may have been written around the beginning of the thirteenth century. Some of the poems in the story may be even older.

Both Halli and Thjodolf are listed among Harald's skalds in the *Skáldatal* (Poets List). Thjodolf Arnorson (in this story his father is called Thorljot) was born early in the eleventh century and served as a court skald both with Magnus the Good and Harald Sigurdson. Surviving from Thjodolf's poetry are a poem about Magnus, as well as the poems attributed to him in this story, and a *drápa* on Harald, called *Sextefja*. Aside from this story and his mention in *Skáldatal*, little is known of Halli.

Just as *Króka Refs saga* was unique in its own way, extolling the virtue of practical wisdom, so is this story unique in Old Icelandic literature as a tale whose protagonist is a jester figure, a laughable but clever buffoon. It is not without forethought that the author of this story reminds his readers of Harald's tolerance of good-natured insult before the story of Halli really begins. From the opening scene to the last, Halli walks a precarious balance between Harald's sense of propriety and his appreciation of wit. This tension is perhaps most evident in the very center of the story. There, after a number of references to Harald's annoying habit of clearing the table before the men have eaten, the author has Halli, in a poem, tender Harald one of the gravest of insults to a Norse king, that he is stingy in feeding his men. Harald's response is a sentence of death, unless Halli can extricate himself in a tour de force of skaldship, by composing a poem on the roasted boar with almost no time to prepare. That Halli can do this, and in the process twit Harald for his kitchen's having burned the nose of the animal, is certainly a compelling display of skill, and once again Harald's appreciation of wit in a man overcomes his sense of propriety. Halli gets off with his life and the roast.

If that is perhaps the incident where Halli comes closest to overstepping the line with Harald, there are others in the remaining parts of the story where it seems clear that Halli, for his wit and buffoonery, enjoys a special relationship with Harald. In the incident with Einar the Fly, for example, in his appreciation of Halli's clever ploy, Harald does not hesitate to alienate Einar, his friend, and one of the most powerful men in Norway. Nor does Harald, later, bend even to the counsel of his own wife where Halli is concerned. The value of Halli to Harald is less certainly in his skaldship than in the general merriment he can produce. Clearly, Thjodolf is the better skald, even Halli admits as much at one point. But Thjodolf provides a clever foil for Halli, being just about everything Halli is not. Thjodolf is zealous in his concern for deportment and defensive of his position as head skald. He avers that a quarreling tanner and smith are not fitting poetical subjects early in the story, while at the story's end Halli will make a poem on an obscene horse. Thjodolf is a man of humble origins, and no doubt is extremely sensitive to that. Halli, when provoked by Thjodolf's charge that he failed to avenge his father, homes in on that sensitivity with unerring aim, telling the amusing story of how Thjodolf's poverty-stricken father met his end. This rivalry with Thjodolf along with Halli's interaction with Harald are the two mainsprings of this story, a tale which looks with affection if not approbation on its hero.

Gull-Ásu-þórðar þáttr

Gull-Asu-þórðar þáttr (The Story of Gold-Asa-Thord) is a short narrative probably written in the third decade of the thirteenth century. It survives in two versions, one independent and one found in Sigurðar saga Jórsalfara in Morkinskinna. This translation is made from the independent version, found in a paper manuscript AM 518, 4to, dating from the seventeenth century. The edition used is that of Jon Johannesson, Íslenzk fornrit, xi (1950), pp. 337-49. All the characters of the story have an independent existence elsewhere in the literature except Asa and Thord. Thord, however, is mentioned in the *Skáldatal* as having composed poetry for Vidkun.

This story is partly about the success of an impoverished Icelander who betters his lot by means of a judicious alliance and astute trading. It also illustrates, somewhat humorously if one looks at it with an eye to Ingimar's predicament, the importance of reciprocity in this society. Vidkun helps Thord because he is indebted to him for the poem. Sigurd helps Vidkun because he has yet to pay back Vidkun's earlier assistance when the Finns attacked his home, and the King helps Sigurd for the assistance Sigurd once rendered his father. It is this reciprocity, which Thord sets in motion at Asa's urging, that enables the marriage to take place and ultimately causes Thord to be accepted in the society.

Bandamanna saga:

Probably written sometime in the third quarter of the thirteenth century, *Bandamanna saga* (The Saga of the Oath-Bound Men) survives in two versions which differ considerably in length and phrasing. This translation is made from the shorter version preserved in the fifteenth century vellum, *Konungsbok* (Gl. kgl. saml. 2845, 4to). The other version is preserved in the fourteenth century vellum, *Möðruvallabók* (AM 132, fol.). The relationship between these two versions and the literary merit of each have been much debated, but without a consensus emerging. There have been several translations of the *Möðruvallabók* version, the most recent of which is Herman Palsson's *The Confederates and Hen Thorir* (The New Saga Library) Edinburgh: Southside, 1975. The edition used in this translation of the Konungsbok version is that of Guðni Jónsson, in *Íslenzk fornrit*, vii (1936), pp. 291-363.

Most of the characters in this saga were historical, and the time frame of the saga can be dated to the middle of the eleventh century, though the central event is not corroborated by other sources. There is a partial analogue, *Ölkofra þáttr*, which recounts the breaking of a lawsuit brought forward by a group of chieftains, but no definite relationship between this story and the Bandamanna saga can be drawn. Odd Ofeigson also has an independent existence in another short story, Odds þáttr Ófeigsson, in which he appears as a clever trader who manages to conceal some illegal trading with the Finns from Harald Sigurdson.

The center of the comedy in the Bandamanna saga is the opposition between the shrewd and witty Ofeig, so astute in the perception of human frailties, and the greedy, grasping chieftains, blinded by their own avarice and pride. This opposition builds until it is released in the hilarity of the exposure scene in the final pages of the saga. There, in some of the most humorous dialogue in all the Family Sagas, the chieftains are publicly disgraced, and Ofeig triumphs. The old order has collapsed, and the new one, properly, starts with a marriage, and the saga ends with a complete reconciliation between Odd and his father, Ofeig.

The concerns of the blood feud are almost peripheral to this saga. Of course, it is Vali's death at the hands of Ospak that brings everyone to the Althing, but this saga does not proceed with the same panoply of consequences and motifs that follow a killing as do other sagas. Rather, it develops the comical opposition between Ofeig and the chieftains. Only at the very end of the saga, in a kind of epilogue, is the subject of the original revenge, Ospak, returned to. And even there it seems more the saga's purpose just to satisfy the reader's curiosity about the fate of this character than to develop him within the context of the blood feud. Much more integral to the epicenter of this saga than the blood feud, it seems, is the estrangement of Ofeig and Odd, father and son. This is the note the story begins on, and the one it ends on. The original reasons for the estrangement are given obliquely. The saga says only that, "Ofeig, his father, was cold to him and loved him little" (105). But it is clear there are considerable differences in temperament between the two. Ofeig, for instance, is portrayed as being financially very conservative, his estate being almost entirely the land he worked, for the reason, the saga says, that "he was not at ease in money matters"(105). His son, however, is of a different nature altogether. He is a precocious entrepreneur, quite willing to risk his capital, and much of the earlier part of the saga develops this side of his character by a strong emphasis on his successful business ventures. There is also a kind of headstrong willfulness to Odd's nature that contrasts pointedly with the unimpulsive, more calculating nature of his father. This is brought out most forcefully in the differences in approach of both men to the manslaughter suit. Unconcerned with detail, and perhaps a bit blinded by an exaggerated assessment of his own power, Odd carelessly prepares his case against Ospak. His father, however, under no such illusions, and prepared with a thorough knowledge of the applicable law, is able to conclude the case successfully.

The depth of this estrangement between father and son is indicated very often in the earlier part of the saga. After Odd's first commercial success with the fishermen, the saga reminds us that, "All this while Odd never went to visit his father, and they both acted as if they weren't kinsmen" (106). Later on, after Odd's trading ventures, we find that Odd now "had more money than most men and he always helped his neighbors, but he never gave help or comfort to Ofeig" (107). The next reference to the estrangement does not come until after the introduction of Ospak, but it is a crucial one, providing the structural climax of the story. By this time Ospak has done well in his work for Odd, well enough apparently, that Odd feels he can leave the farm in his hands while he and Vali go out trading. The problem is the chieftainship. Odd must find someone to maintain it in his absence. He chooses Ospak, a crucial decision, and the events of the remainder of the saga all develop from it. The logical choice, however, is his own father, as even Ospak, himself, points out to Odd. He says, "There's no one more fitted for this than your father, a most wise and trustworthy man" (109). There follows immediately the reference to the estrangement, "Odd said he wouldn't put it in his father's hands" (109). He gives it to Ospak, and the unfortunate consequences of this decision occupy the remainder of the saga. The choice of a relatively unknown character of doubtful reputation over his own father to guard his interests surely indicates the great depth of the estrangement between father and son, and this climactic point in the saga no doubt also indicates the nadir of their relationship, for after this point the relationship gradually improves Ofeig breaks the silence, takes up Odd's case against

Ospak successfully, and later, just before the countersuit by the chieftains, the saga indicates of the father and son that, "things got better between them" (120). Ofeig then proceeds to help his son and breaks the conspiracy, exposing all his enemies, and in the process, arranging a suitable match for Odd. While the saga does not overtly indicate a total abatement of the estrangement, it ends on a note suggesting that this has, in fact, happened. "Odd remained a powerful man," the saga concludes, and, "He had a son and named him Ofeig" (135).

Gísls þáttr Illugasonar:

Gísls þáttr Illugasonar (The Story of Gisl Illugason) was probably written in the first decade of the thirteenth contury. It is preserved in a fourteenth century vellum, AM 66, fol. and a fifteenth century vellum, Gl. kgl. saml. 1010, fol. The differences between the two texts are minimal. The story, or at least a much changed version of it, is also found in an insert in both versions of *Jóns saga helga*. The relationships between the *þáttr* and the inserts are unclear. It may be that the author of the *þáttr* was reworking the inserts, or vice versa, or even more likely that both versions depend on some other source. The *Jóns saga helga* version of the story has been translated into English by Jacqueline Simpson in *The Northmen Talk*, Madison: Univ. of Wisconsin Press, 1965, pp. 65-70. There are radical differences between this version of the story and the þáttr. This translation of the *þáttr* is made from the edition of Sigurður Nordal in *Íslenzk fornrit*, iii (1938), pp. 329-42, an edition based on AM 66.

Gisl Illugason lived around the beginning of the twelfth century. He is named in the *Skáldatal* among the skalds of Magnus Bareleg. Of his poetry a *drápa* praising Magnus written in 1104 and the occasional verse in this *þáttr* survive. As to the historicity of the events of this story we have only the two vastly different versions of it from which to judge.

This story is thought by many to be among the best of the shorter narratives. Clearly, it was written more in the heroic spirit and less in the mode of hagiography as is the other version in _Jóns saga helga_. Nonetheless, a very strong spirit of reconciliation seems evident in this story, a spirit which is foreign to the older narratives. Gjafvald's last words to Harald, in which he absolves Gisl, are in this vein, as are, of course, Jon's words to Harald at the Thing. The vengeance thirsty Sigurd has a complete change of heart by the end of the story, and even Harald is mollified finally by a combination of Jon's words and Gisl's actions. However, the story also preserves the traditional heroic virtues. Gisl, only seventeen when he arrives in Norway, very boldly avenges the death of his father. He nobly clears Thorstein of any complicity in the slaying, and he faces his own death with stoic disdain. It is unusual in Old Icelandic literature that such a unified mixture of the older heroic virtue and Christian reconciliation is achieved, and it is probably just this balance that gives the tale much of its appeal.

Bjarnar saga Hítdoelakappa:

Bjarnar saga Hítdoelakappa (The Saga of Bjorn, Champion of Hitardale) is one of the few sagas that survive only in fragments. Chief among these fragments are two paper manuscripts, AM 551 Da, 4to, and Rask 28, dating from the seventeenth and eighteenth centuries respectively. A portion of the saga is also found in AM 162, fol., a fourteenth century vellum known as _Skinnbókarbrot_. The original beginning of this saga was lost before these copies were made; however, a fairly reliable redaction of the original introductory chapters was later found intercalated in _Olafs saga helga_. This redaction, found in AM 71, fol. _(Baejarbók)_ and AM 488, 4to, serves as the text for the beginning of this translation (up to the fourth paragraph of the fifth chapter). The edition used in this translation is that of Sigurðr Nordal and Guðni Jonsson, in _Íslenzk fornrit_, iii, 1938, pp.111-211.

Bjarnar saga is thought to be among the oldest of the Family Sagas. It was probably first written down in the first decade or so of the thirteenth century, although the events it purports to chronicle cover the last decade of the tenth century and the first quarter of the eleventh. The saga recounts the lives of Bjorn Arngeirson and his lifelong enemy, Thord Kolbeinson. Both characters appear to have some historical basis, though little is known about either outside of *Bjarnar saga*. Thord was some fifteen years older than Bjorn, and he was a skald at the court of Jarl Eirikr Hakonarson during the second decade of the eleventh century. Some fragments of two works he composed there (*Belgskakadrápa* and *Eiriksdrápa*)) survive, but most of his surviving poetry is preserved in *Bjarnar saga*. One of Thord's sons, Arnorr, became one of the best skalds of this period.

None of Bjorn's poetry survives outside of *Bjarnar saga*, and there is even some doubt about the authenticity of the verses attributed to him in the saga. The text of the poems is quite corrupt, and the narrative and the poems correlate not at all well with one another. Nonetheless, *Bjarnar saga* is unique among the other sagas in this collection in that it is the life story of a poet. In this respect it is similar to those four other sagas whose subject is also the life of a skald: *Egil's saga*; *Kormak's saga*; *Hallfred's saga*; and *Gunnlaug's saga*.

Bjarnar saga also has fairly close affinities to one of the greatest of all the Icelandic sagas, *Laxdoela*. While *Laxdoela* has a complexity and grandeur that *Bjarnar saga* lacks, the essence of both sagas is a searching concern with the complexities of human love. There are, of course, obvious comparisons, such as in *Laxdoela* Bolli's return to Iceland and subsequent courtship and winning of Gudrun with Thord's return to Iceland and subsequent betrayal of Bjorn in order to win Oddny. However, such structural similarities only reflect the deeper concerns of both sagas. One could say that the real story in *Laxdoela* is Gudrun's. Almost all the external conflict in that saga revolves around her, or rather, her very complex relationship with Kjartan, her former lover and Bolli, her husband. When, near the end of the saga, she answers the question of whom she loved the most with the famous response, "I was worst to him I loved the most," she is articulating in a way the most elemental concern of the saga, the power of human love.

Certainly, in *Bjarnar saga*, Oddny has not the complexity of Gudrun, nor in any but the most trivial way can the main story of the saga be said to be hers. It is clearly the saga of Bjorn Arngeirson, the Champion of Hitardale. And yet, like *Laxdoela*, the mainspring of the action in the story is the power of human love. Bjorn never stopped loving, or indeed, it appears, even seeing Oddny. It is also clear from Oddny's response to Bjorn's death that she shared this love. It is a far greater and more fitting punishment that Thord suffers in this final and complete alienation of Oddny than even the catastrophic fines he suffers in the final settlement. It is the final humiliating recognition that throughout his life he really had Oddny in name only.

While this love story rides below the surface in this saga, it is never far below. In the beginning of the middle section of the saga, when Bjorn has agreed to winter with Thord, it is Thord's slapping of Oddny that starts the exchange of insult-poems. The exchange is intensified with Thord's provoking Bjorn by openly displaying affection to Oddny, and this first exchange ends with Bjorn referring obliquely in a verse to his continuing sexual relationship with Oddny. These verses precipitate the cycle of feuding that occupies the middle section of the saga.

After these initial stages of the feud, Chapters 13-20, in which the consequences of this frustrated love are played out, the saga again reminds the reader at a very central position in the saga of the underlying mainspring for all the action. In Chapter 21, in an otherwise irrevelant digression about one of Thord's sons, Kolli, the reader is again reminded obliquely of the powerful attraction of Bjorn for Oddny.

In the last half of the saga, the feud runs its inexorable course until the final ambush. There again, this time not with oblique allusions but with bitter, forceful irony, the saga reminds its readers what caused and what perpetuated this feud. The hardest and most ferocious of Bjorn's attackers turns out to be unwitting Kolli, Bjorn's own son by Oddny.

In the aftermath of Bjorn's beheading, in the dramatic scenes of the announcement of the slaying, the saga again points not to a motiveless enmity between two men, but to a love that never ended. Bjorn's wife, Thordis, herself obviously no stranger to Bjorn's affection for Oddny, throws Bjorn's necklace back at Thord, bidding him take it to Oddny as a "keepsake." So also Bjorn's mother bids Thord take Bjorn's head back to Oddny, as "It will seem better to her than that wretched little head which dangles from your neck!"

Especially at the end of this saga, excepting the promulgation of the final settlement, is the reader reminded of the cause of all the feuding. It is a poignant moment when Thord admits he would rather choose death than suffer Oddny's alienation, that what he sought to protect for so long he lost irrevocably in the end, and perhaps, though the saga is ambiguous on this point, never really had at all. At the end, Thord thinks it only "a great sorrow that Bjorn's and his and Oddny's paths had ever crossed."

Bjarnar saga has often been criticised for its apparent uneveness, in particular, for an extensive middle section that sems only to recount local tradition without any firm connection to the beginning or end. In its defense, however, one could say of the saga that it does have a unity, though not perhaps in its presentation of external action. Its unity lies in the cause of the external action, the force and power of the love of two men for one woman.

SAGA OF CLEVER REF

Chapter 1---Thorbjorn and Stein

In the days of King Hakon, Athelstan's foster son, a man called Stein lived out in Iceland in Breidafjord on a farm called Kvennabrek.[1] His wife was named Thorgerd. She was Oddleif's daughter and the sister of Gest from Bardastrand. Stein was a wealthy man and the best of householders, but he was also very old. He had a son called Ref.[2]

Ref was handsome to look at. He had grown very large at an early age, and he wasn't easy to deal with. No man knew his strength. He was also quite an idler, and usually had nothing better to do than get in the way of busy people. It seemed a great pity to Stein and Thorgerd that their son should be so different from others. By most men he was called a fool.

There was a man called Thorbjorn. He was rich and not easy to deal with, a great fighter, but the most unjust of men. He had owned land on all four Quarters of Iceland, but chieftains as well as common folk had kicked him out each time, for his slayings and wrongdoing. He had paid compensation to no one. His wife was Rannveig, a foolish and bossy woman, and it was said that Thorbjorn would have withstood less bad luck, had she not stirred him up. Now Thorbjorn had bought the land called Sandafell, and many men were greatly worried about his coming -- at least those who knew about him before.

It was not far from Stein's farm to Thorbjorn's, and a brook ran between the farms. It divided their lands. After Thorbjorn had lived there awhile, he took his sheep to graze on Stein's land. He had a lot of livestock. Soon Stein went to speak with his neighbor, Thorbjorn, and he said to him, "You have now farmed near me for two years, and there has been more good than ill between us, though you are said to be an unfriendly man. Up to this time I've not had any trouble from you or your livestock, but now you let your sheep graze in my pastures. I wish that after this talk you would change and mind your sheep better than you have. I'm not known to be a liar, and I know men would believe my words, especially those who have quarreled with you before. But I could also say that you have shown me no unfairness, or wished to do me any wrong."

Thorbjorn said no one had ever talked so wisely or gently with him, and it made him think that if more had talked so decently to him, he would have killed less often, and he added, "I shall certainly do better after this talk."

After this, they parted, and Thorbjorn changed so much due to Stein's talk that his livestock never did any damage to Stein again.

Chapter 2--Thorgerd's Troubles

Later on, Stein fell ill. He allowed as how he wasn't likely to catch any more illnesses, since this one was surely enough for his death. He said to Thorgerd, his wife,"I want you to sell the land after my death and go west to your brother Gest in Bardastrand. Tell him it is my feeling that Thorbjorn will trouble you before long, even though it has gone well between us up to now. I think he will likely cause grazing problems as he did before." Soon after that Stein died.

Some time passed, and Thorgerd decided not to part with the land, for it seemed very good to her, and fair. Quite a bit later, though, Thorbjorn's sheep tending began to grow worse. So bad did it become that all the turf was chewed up, and for two years her livestock died from lack of hay. Thorgerd often talked to Thorbjorn about it, that he should mind the sheep better, but it didn't help. So she looked about for someone to buy her land, but no one was eager to settle so near Thorbjorn. Thus the land was not sold.

It is said that there was a man in the district named Bard. He was the smallest of men so he was called Bard the Little. He was also the swiftest of men, and he could run as fast as the best of horses. He was sharp-sighted and quick-witted, and he was faithful and true in all things. In the summers, he tended livestock.

Thorgerd met Bard at the spring Thing, and she asked him if he would oversee her property. She said he would get a deal that pleased him, but she told him he would often need to guard against Thorbjorn's sheep, and she told him all, for better or worse, what working the household between them would mean.

Bard said, "I would choose to be no other place than with you from what you say. It doesn't seem very hard to me to defend your land against the pasturage of another man."

Bard then went home with Thorgerd and began sheep tending. He made two sheds for himself, one on the hillside and one on the bank of the stream which ran between the farms. He always spent the night at that hut and guarded Thorgerd's land from Thorbjorn's sheep so that they couldn't cross the stream. He stood on the bank and turned them back. But he never crossed the stream.

Chapter 3---Ref's Revenge

Thorgerd's livestock now began to milk well. That had not happened in the last summer. But to the housewife Rannveig the summer milking seemed a little less. One day she talked with Thorbjorn and asked where he grazed the stock. He said they grazed every day along the stream.

"How can it happen," she said, "that this man with Thorgerd forbids our stock the pasture they had last summer? Your hands are mislaid, Thorbjorn, when you come to blows with all those innocent men, but let this stupid man dishonor us by forbidding our sheep the pasture they want."

"Who is this man? said Thorbjorn.

"His name is Bard," said Rannveig, "and he is the smallest and poorest of men. Every night he lies out and keeps our stock from coming across the river."

Whereupon Thorbjorn took his horse and rode across the stream.

Bard was in the shed when he got there, Thorbjorn said to him, "Is is true that you keep our stock from this pasture and fix it so they dare not eat near the river? We have gotten no milk from the stock."

Bard said, "It's no lie that I never let your stock in here, but it's not true that I beat your stock or keep them from your own land. I hope you haven't any less this summer than last, but if that's so, then it has justly come to you."

Thorbjorn said, "It seems more likely to me that you have done wrong than I, and you'll be called a robber if anything unforseen turns up at the fall roundup. You better stop what you're doing now, or else you'll come to grief."

Bard said, "Always before in this way have I kept faithful service as a herd tender, and so it shall be now."

Thorbjorn then struck Bard his death blow and dragged him into the shed. After that, he rode home and told what he had done. Rannveig thought well of what happened and at once had the livestock driven into Thorgerd's land. The stock went into the home meadow, tore up her pasture, and did great harm. Thorgerd came out and saw the stock standing around all over the yard. She knew what trouble this meant. She got men to drive the livestock away, and they found Bard slain in the shed. They told Thorgerd about it. She went into the kitchen where she found her son, Ref.

She said to him, "My mind always shudders when I see you before my eyes--such a shame to your family. What an unlucky woman I was, to give birth to one so witless. A daughter would have been better. Then, at least, I could have gotten her a man who be of some help to us. Though our farm is torn up, our home meadow ruined, and a man slain, you still lie there in your laziness and act as if we can do nothing about it."

Ref then stood up and said, "More rebukes from you, Mother, will surely be hard to bear, if these first ones are so bad."

He took down a spear-ax. Stein had kept many weapons.

Ref then left the yard and went along by throwing the spear out in front of him and running up after it. Thorbjorn's housemen were at work and saw Ref going along this way. They saw who it was and made great fun of him. Ref made for Thorbjorn's house, and when he got to the door, he saw no men around. He heard women in the building, talking about whether Thorbjorn should be awakened. He had laid down to sleep. Ref then broke the shaft from his spear, went in quickly, and crossed the floor. Thorbjorn heard him and asked who was out there.

Ref said, "It's me."

"Who are you?" said Thorbjorn.

"A man from another farm," said Ref.

"You must have a name, though," said Thorbjorn.

"Ref is my name!" he said, and jumped right into the bedroom.

Thorbjorn was undressed and he said, "I must be getting feeble not to know who you were. Welcome, Ref, and what is your business here?"

Ref said, "What it will be greatly depends on you."

"How is that?" said Thorbjorn.

Ref said, "I've come to ask for compensation for the slaying of my houseman, Bard. I'll be content with as little as you care to give, as long as it satisfies my honor. It will honor me if you heed my charge that you have slain a poor man."

Thorbjorn now began to dress quickly and he said, "It's right for you to ask for this, and it may be that I will pay in this case, unlike all the others."

Ref said, "It is fitting for you to pay something for this."

Thorbjorn said, "Since you speak so well about this, something shall be paid for it." He was now dressed and he reached down behind the bedpost and picked up a large knife, made wholly of iron, and a whetstone. He pulled them out and passed the knife and whetstone to Ref and he said, "Soft things for the soft of heart." At that, Ref thrust the spear into Thorbjorn's belly.[3] Thorbjorn fell back and he couldn't get the knife drawn in time. It was fastened to its sheath, and it all happened too quickly. Ref then closed the bedroom door and started for the main door, closing the sitting room door at the same time. Outside, by the men's door was a large pile of driftwood.[4] Ref decided to hide in the woodpile, because he knew he couldn't get home without being seen by Thorbjorn's men.

The women had heard Ref and Thorbjorn talking and they wondered about it. Then they saw blood running along the floor. They called for the housemen, and when the men came, they found Thorbjorn slain. They looked for Ref, but they didn't find him. Though no one had seen Ref go home, they still gave up the search in the evening, and Ref then got out of the woodpile and went home.

He woke his mother and asked her to come outside. As soon as she had done so, she asked whether Thorbjorn had paid any compensation for the slaying of Bard. Ref said:

Broad knife and whetstone
Offered me today
By a sea-fire gatherer (sea-fire=gold; gold gatherer=man)
Would never be enough.
With my viper of wounds (spear)
I sought the heart-path (chest)
Of the Hord-giver (man)
And killed him.

"Your words are most welcome," she said, "Get the two horses out in the yard and bring them to me." A saddle was then laid on one, but the other was made to carry a sack with costly treasures inside. Ref then put on good clothes, and he looked like a most worthy young man.

Thorgerd said, "There is a man named Grim who lives a short way down the valley on our land. He shall be your guide, for I'm sending you west to Bardastrand to Gest, my brother. I want you to stay there until this slaying is settled."

Chapter 4--Ref Builds a Ship

Ref went on his way and didn't stop before he got to Hagi. There he got a good welcome, and when he met his kinsman, Gest, he was asked for the news. Ref said he had nothing to tell.

"Don't you have anything to tell?" asked Gest. Ref said that maybe he had something of note and told him, then, what had happened. Gest said certainly he would keep him and asked if he had any skills. Ref said he was far from being skilled in any way.

Gest said, "I believe that in some way you are a very skilled man, and I will soon find out what it is." Ref stayed there for some time.

Some time later on Gest came to speak with Ref and he said, "Now I know your skill. You could be a master craftsman, if only you wanted to. I'll bet that if you took up the thread-winding stick, you would wind neither crosswise, nor upside-down, nor unevenly, but you would do it with great agility --

if you would only try it."

"That may be," said Ref, "but I've never done such craft work before."

Gest said, "I want you to try. In fact, I want you to make me a seal-hunting boat."

Whereupon Ref said, "Get me the tools and stuff to do it with, and more than enough, for men say if something turns out poorly, it usually was poorly fitted out to start with. Also, I want no one to know about this, for then it would be said that if it turned out well, someone must have helped me and taught me how to do it."

So, Gest had a large ship-shed built, and brought much wood to it. A trading ship had broken up on Gest's beach, and he bought all the ship's timbers. All this wood Gest had carried to Ref's ship-shed, and all the nails too. Gest also had some unworked iron, and Ref wanted that too, saying he wanted to strike the nails himself. Gest then had a forge and charcoal carried there and all manner of smith's tools.

At last Gest said, "Now I've had everything brought to your shed, and you won't lack the least thing, all so that here might be built a ship that could well sail the open sea."

Ref said that no matter how the work should turn out, he surely could have done no more.

Ref began to work. He rose early and came home late, and this went on for three months. Then one morning Gest sent his most trustworthy man to the ship-shed. He asked him to find out how the ship-building was going. Gest said he thought it should be done by now, even though Ref knew very little about boat building. The man went and watched without Ref's knowing. He looked very carefully at the work. Then he went home and told Gest that men would not often see such a seal-boat as this one, and he added, "For a greater ship than this has never come to Iceland!"

Gest bade him be quiet about it, and two more months passed.

Chapter 5--Ref meets Gellir

One morning after Gest had been up awile, he found Ref still lying in his bed. Gest shook him and said, "You sleep long, kinsman. Is the seal-boat done now?"

"It can be said," answered Ref, "that it should float now, and I shall do no more before you see it."

"Then we shall go today," said Gest, "and see this work."

Gest went to the ship-shed at once, but with only a few men, since he didn't want everyone to know if the boat were poorly made. When he got there, he saw a most seaworthy trading ship. Gest looked closely at this ship and greatly admired its workmanship, and all the more since Ref had not made a ship before. He thanked Ref for the ship and said, "Now I wish to reward you for this ship. I want to give it to you."

Ref said he would eagerly accept it.

The news spread widely that Ref Steinson had made a seaworthy trading ship, and that seemed most surprising news, for he was still thought by many to be a fool. But it so happened that a long time ago a Norwegian and his son had been staying with Ref's father. They were the same age, the Norwegian's son and Ref. The son had a toy ship that was in every way just like a seaworthy Norwegian trading ship, and before the boy left, he gave the ship to Ref. Ref used to pass the time in the kitchen by taking it apart.

Soon the winter began, and the time for games came. There was a man called Gellir, a great sea trader who spent every other year in Norway. He was a great boaster and much taken to sports. His mother, Sigrid, was very wealthy and lived a short way away from Hlid. Her husband was dead, and thus Gellir was called Sigrid's son. Gellir often went to the games, and he was the strongest person there. One day Gellir was on his way with some others to the games in Hagi. He asked Ref if he wanted to go along. Ref said he wasn't fit for games and told him he wouldn't go. Gellir asked if Ref would at least wrestle with him. Ref said he wouldn't. Gellir then leaped from his horse, ran up to Ref and said, "No one has ever refused me, and we're going to wrestle now whether you want to or not!"

He then tried many ways to bring Ref down, but he couldn't make him fall. No matter how hard Gellir held him, Ref always slipped out. When Gellir wearied a bit, Ref grabbed his belt with one hand, put the other between his shoulders, and threw him down on the frozen ground a short way away. Gellir came down on his elbows, broke both of them, and bruised his forehead. He sprang up quickly, grabbed his spear, raised it aloft, and threw it at Ref. It glanced off his chest and struck his head, but he wasn't sorely hurt by it. Gellir and his friends then ran off and boasted about it. They said Gellir had struck Ref two great blows, and that Ref wouldn't take revenge. This news carried widely, but Ref behaved as if he didn't know. Gest had not been home during all this.

Chapter 6--Ref Sails for Greenland

After Yule, Ref tarred his ship and got it ready for sea. Gest supplied all the rigging. It is said that Gellir left home on a trip and his way took him close to Ref's ship-shed. Gellir looked at the ship. One man was with him. When Ref heard Gellir outside, he ran from under the ship with his smith's ax and said, "Now I shall pay back your two blows with one!" The blow hit Gellir's side, and the ax went deep inside. Gellir fell dead on the ground there, and the man who was with him rode away. Ref went home and found Gest.

Gest said, "You look happy, kinsman. What happened?"

Ref said:

Today a troll of shields (ax)
Reddened was in Gellir's blood;
A famous sea-fire bender (sea-fire=gold;

Was slain by my hand gold-bender=man)
Now I've avenged two blows,
And hot blood has the raven.
Such is the stuff
Of the wise tales of old.

"Just as the best of men would do," said Gest, "and I would have done the same when I heard it spread around that Gellir struck you twice and you did nothing about it. But what are you going to do now?

Ref said, "I'm going to sail my ship to Greenland."

Gest said, "You do as I would want you, for you wouldn't be very safe in Norway once they learn of this slaying. Now I'll supply your ship with a crew and get you as much money as you want, and later we'll settle things for your mother as best we can."

Ref got his ship ready and chose brave farmers' sons to go with him. Gest did well by him, and at parting he said to Ref, "If fate does not allow you to come back here, then I want you to have a saga written about your journey. It will be thought by many to be worthy of note, for I know you're the smartest of all our kinsmen. Also, good things will happen to you. I pray that He who made the sun now grant you good luck."

Ref thanked Gest well for his good words.

So they parted, and Ref set out to sea. They fared well until they sighted Greenland. Then they were tossed about for a long time and driven north along the coast. After a while they came to a fjord far to the north in the wilderness. Glaciers came all the way out to the sea, but because they were weary from the storm, they were eager to land.

They cast out an anchor, and Ref rowed to land. He then climbed the highest hill to look around. He saw that the fjord cut a long way back into the land from where they were, but that there was a headland on each side that seemed to block it off.

In the morning, he had his men bring the ship in to where the fjord seemed to end. When they got to the headlands, they saw that the fjord went on beyond them for a long way, and when they got to the real end of the fjord, they found a good harbor. Woods grew on all the hillsides and green slopes, and the harbor was surrounded by glaciers. There were a great many animals, and driftwood lay all over the shore. There were plenty of fish to catch. They need go no further. They built a large hall, fixed it up well, and there they spent the winter. Ref built a large ferry and made it ready to sail to the settlement.[5]

In the spring he loaded it with trading goods, and they sailed to the settlement. They landed in a little bay. A short way up from the bay stood a farmhouse where a man called Bjorn lived. He was married and had one daughter, named Helga. She was pretty and skillful, and thought to be the best match in the settlement. Ref didn't sell his wares, but instead began to do woodwork. Bjorn met Ref and asked if he would work for him and make his house larger. Ref agreed, and they worked out a deal. Ref went to work on the house and made it very large indeed. From then on the farm was called Hlid.

On the other side of the headland stood a farm called Vik. A man named Thorgil lived there, but he was called Bald Vik. He was spiteful, slanderous but cagey, and very cruel. Everyone thought it no good to have anything to do with him. He was married and very old. His sons were Thengil, the oldest, then Orm, Thorstein, and Geir. He had a daughter named Olof, and she was married to a man nammed Gunnar. Thengil had proposed to Helga, but she didn't want to marry him.

By this time, Ref was staying with Bjorn's household, and he asked for Helga's hand. Bjorn happily agreed. Thormod, Helga's foster brother, also agreed. He was so eager the match take place that he made ready the wedding feast. They all agreed on these terms, that Ref and Helga would live at Hlid. Bjorn would give up the house, but would still live there with them.

The following spring Ref took up householding there and quickly prospered. He made a lot of money woodworking. Helga was also very good at overseeing the farm. When they had been there only a short time, Bjorn died. Soon after, Ref and Helga had a child, a son they named Stein. Two years later they had another, named Bjorn. The two brothers were most promising young boys.

Ref lived at this homestead for eight years. During this time he began work on a large ferry. The ship-shed for it was out on this headland which went between Vik and Hlid. He always went to the shed early and stayed late, and he always locked his smith's ax in the shed for the night and went home unarmed.

Chapter 7--Ref and the Thorgilsons' Slander

One afternoon while he went home in his usual manner, Ref looked far up the headland and saw a white bear. The bear trotted away when he saw the man. Ref remembered he was unarmed. New snow was on the ground, and the tracks would be clear wherever the bear went, so Ref saw no reason to go after the bear weaponless. He went back to the ship-shed and then returned to where the bear had been. It was dead. The Thorgilson brothers had killed it when they came home from rowing. Ref went home.

When the Thorgilsons got home, they began talking. Their father asked what they had caught. They said they had caught no fish, but they added, "We got you a white bear!"

Thorgil said, "Your help is great, when you so supply our household. Few could have done what you did."

Thengil said, "We would have gotten little from this fishing trip had not that coward Ref showed his true mettle. I think a more gutless person has never come to Greenland. His tracks led away from the ship-shed, then right back to it -- and there was urine splattered all over them!" Thengil then went on to speak much unlawful slander against Ref. Thorgil, his father, was silent. Thengil asked why he was silent.

"Is it that you don't know who the coward Ref is, father?" he said.

Thorgil answered, "About such it is sickening to speak. Always must Greenland blush to hear of Ref. I have seen that ever since he came here, he has only earned for Greenland the greatest shame. I've had little to do with him, for I've heard that when he was in Iceland, his nature was not like other men's. He was a women every ninth night and needed a man.[6] For this he was called Ref the Unmanly, and there were always stories of his strange doings. Now I want you to have nothing to do with him."

They then broke off their talk and began to butcher the bear, but thereafter, wherever the Thorgilsons went, they carried on this slander and told everyone this rumor, that Ref had been forced from Iceland for his unmanliness, and had even been given money to stay away. They told this slander to so many that it became common talk, and Ref happened to hear about it. He didn't let on that he knew, but he fitted out the ship he had been working on with the best rigging he could find.

In the fall he slaughtered many cattle, and also sold some for Greenland wares. Ref then held a great autumn feast and asked his friends to his home, but quietly he sold his land. He had decided to leave the land within the year and he made this known at the feast where he had with him many brave men, no less than twelve. This was at the double month.[7]

Chapter 8--Ref's Revenge

One day Thormod came to speak with Ref and he said, "Nearly all the common folk think poorly of you, and this was all started by Thorgil and his sons. When we favored your marriage to Helga, we thought to give her a stalwart man, and so we thought you. But now it begins to look like you are proving the words of wicked men when you sit around so quietly. I ask you now to charge them with this slander."

Ref said, "A man should first have some plan in mind before doing risky things--or before he urges others to do them."

Then they broke off their talk. Ref sat down to work and made an unusually large spear. With it he could slash as well as thrust. He made it with a short shaft which he wound all the way up with iron, then he sharpened it so it could split a hair.

Later in the day Ref left home, alone. He was armed with only the spear. He went towards Vik and got there very late in the afternoon. Thorgil was cooking in the kitchen. Ref went there. Thorgil asked who was there. Ref gave his name.

Thorgil said, "I must be getting old not to recognize you. You are most welcome."

Ref said, "I am glad."

Thorgil said, "What do you have in mind?"

Ref said, "I have come to ask compensation for your slander of me."

Thorgil said, "When have we spoken poorly of you, and what is this slander that you say we have done?"

Ref told him.

Thorgil said, "I don't deny that we spoke many words in jest, but they cannot be called lies, for I believed them to be true!"

Ref struck him then with the spear and cleaved him down to the shoulders. He quickly drew the spear out and went down to the shore to look for Thorgil's sons in the boathouse.

By now it was pitch-dark. All of a sudden he heard oars splashing. The brothers had come to land. Thengil leaped ashore and went up to look for the launch rollers. When he got near, Ref hewed off his head. Then Thorstein leaped ashore, but he didn't know what had happened since it was so dark he couldn't see the boathouse. Thorstein picked up the oars and carried them up to the boathouse, and when he got to the door, Ref thrust the spear through him. At that, Thorstein called out and said, "Save yourselves, boys! Our brother Thorgil is slain, and I am run through!"

They rowed off and down the headland to the place where Ref's ship-shed stood. Thinking that Ref would not look for them there, they landed. But when they had dragged the boat ashore, Ref came up and slew them both.

After that Ref went home and ordered his men to carry both provisions and wares to the ship and to load them on board. It came to be that by dawn all the goods Ref wanted to have with him were loaded on the ship. Ref then rewarded well the young men who had been with him, and he told them to be ready to follow him when he came back, whenever that might be. They eagerly agreed to this. Ref then sent a message to the buyers of his land that they could now take it over. At last Ref boarded the ship with his wife and sons. Stein was then nine years old, and Bjorn, seven. Thormod was the third son, and he was three. Helga's foster brother, Thormod, would also go with them. The wind came off the land, and they hoisted the sail. That day they sailed out to sea. For a while now they are out of this saga.

Chapter 9--Gunnar Searches for Ref

The first thing that happened was the housemen's finding the slain Thorgil, and then in the evening when they went to the shore, they found the slain Thengil and Thorstein. The next morning they found the other two. The news spread widely, but neither Thorgil nor his sons got much pity. Many thought it was quite a feat for one man to have done all that in a single night, and they thought Ref had avenged himself for the slander not without vigor.

When Gunnar, Thorgil's kinsman, heard this news, he wanted to have a watchtower built on the headlands of both Greenland settlements in case Ref should land at either place in the autumn, but he couldn't get the land for this because it was all sold. Gunnar then took men into the West Settlement, but he learned nothing about Ref there. In the spring, Gunnar sent men into the wilderness to search for Ref, but they didn't find him, and no one had even heard of him. Gunnar then began to think that Ref had been lost at sea, for he had sailed with only six unskilled men. And so passed four years, and since nothing was ever heard of Ref, this searching for him finally stopped. Men thought he had either died or sailed his ship into the wilderness. We shall now turn from this for a while.

Chapter 10--Bard and Gunnar Find Ref

While Ref was growing up and while all this was going on, there had been a great change of rulers in Norway. Now King Harald Sigurdson had come to power.[8] With his men was a man called Bard. He was close to the King. He did summer trading in either Iceland or the Western Lands,[9] and he was to go out this summer we are now talking about. He meant to go to Iceland and he got his ship ready. The King summoned Bard and asked where he meant to sail his ship.

"To Iceland," said Bard.

The King said, "I want you to go somewhere else. You must sail out to Greenland and bring us walrus ivory and hides from there."

Bard said it would be as the King wished.

After that, Bard put to sea and had a trouble-free voyage. When he got to Greenland, he went to stay the winter with Gunnar. When he had been there a while, he brought up this matter. He asked Gunnar if it were true what he had heard, that a single Icelander had slain a father and four sons in one night while avenging himself for the slander they had stirred up about him. Gunnar allowed there was some truth to this. Bard asked what had happened to the man.

"We think," said Gunnar, "he was lost at sea, because he was so afraid that he set sail at the beginning of winter with only six men." Bard asked if anything had happened since. Gunnar told what he knew.

Bard said, "I would be greatly surprised if this man were lost at sea. He has had very good luck in escaping from you, and it seems more likely to me that he is still on the loose. Have you searched the wilderness?"

Gunnar said they had searched everywhere it was likely men might be and then some.

Bard said, "How could he possibly sail in the face of winter with so few men on a lone trading ship? I think it's better you see that revenge for Thorgil and his sons is not going to happen. Nonetheless, early in the spring I want you to have a ship made ready for us. We shall go into the wilderness, and if I don't find him, then I'll have to believe he has surely perished."

Gunnar said it would be so.

The winter passed, and once the ice broke up, Gunnar began his journey. They had seven men on board, and they sailed into the wilderness. They searched each hidden bay, but they didn't find any sign of men, and Bard was a most sharpsighted man.

One evening they came to a great fjord which wound its way crookedly into the land. When they got to its end, they anchored their ship for the night in an inlet. Bard rowed to land in a boat. He went up the headland at the fjord's end, and looked around. The night was bright. A little breeze ran over the fjord. He saw where some seaweed drifted along to the end of the fjord, then suddenly vanished. This surprised Bard greatly, and he went further along the edge of the headland. He saw where another fjord began, wide and long, and there he saw a valley leading up to the mountains, large and beautiful. He then went back to the ship and went to sleep.

In the morning Bard asked whether they had explored the whole fjord. Gunnar said that was so. Bard said he wanted to go to the very end of the fjord. They did so, and came to where the headlands ran together. There was a channel cut between them. It was very narrow and deep. On the other side the fjord opened up and it was very long.

Late in the evening they came to a bay, but the

men were not minded to explore the land, and all went to sleep, exept Bard. Alone, he rowed a boat to land and walked along the shore until he came upon a great pile of wood chips. He picked up some chips and took them back with him to the ship.

In the morning Bard showed Gunnar the chips and said, "Never in my life have I seen wood chips so skillfully cut. Was Ref handy with tools?"

Gunnar said, "He was the greatest of craftsmen."

Bard said, "I think we had better search for Ref as if he were alive."

Then they went ashore with some men. Soon they saw a building standing almost at the edge of the beach. They went over there and walked around it and looked at it carefully. They thought they had never seen such beautiful workmanship. It was large and strongly made, not packed with tar, and very square. Nowhere did they see a joint. It looked as if it were all of one piece. But, as they were looking at it, a man came out of the building. He was very large. He greeted Gunnar, and Gunnar returned the greeting. They knew now that this was Ref.

He asked where they meant to go.

Bard said, "No further than here."

Ref asked for the news. Bard said he would tell him nothing. Ref said that they also would hear no more than he thought fit. Bard then told his men to bring firewood to the building.

When the wood was stacked, they lit the fire. The wood caught fire quickly, but just as quickly it went out. Again they went out for more wood, and then they saw a great stream of water come out of the building and completely put out the fire. They looked all over the building, but they couldn't find where it came from. Then they moved the fire up on top of the building, but no less water came out of there than below.

Ref went out of the building and said, "Is the building hard to overcome?"

Bard said, "You may well brag over your trickery in this, and we shall turn away from you here this time, but I promise you this -- if you dare stay here another spring, Gunnar and I will have your head!"

Ref said, "Though I stay here many more years, neither you nor any of the Greenlanders here will succeed in killing me, unless you use cleverer men than yourself."

Chapter 11--Gifts for King Harald

After that Bard and Gunnar turned back to their ship and sailed towards the settlements. In the autumn they came to the West-Settlement where Bard spent another winter with Gunnar. Next summer Bard got his ship ready for Norway, and Gunnar gave him gifts. Gunnar also sent King Harald three costly things. One was a fully grown but well-tamed white bear. Another treasure was a walrus ivory chess set, made with great workmanship. The third treasure was a walrus skull with both tusks. It was all carved and inlaid with gold. The tusks were fastened to the skull. That was the greatest treasure of all.

Chapter 12--Bard Seeks King Harald's Advice

Bard now put to sea and had a good journey. He made land at the harbor he wanted to and he brought King Harald many choice Greenland wares. One day Bard went before the King and said, "Here is a chess set, lord, which is sent to you by Gunnar, the noblest man in Greenland. He wants no money for it, only your friendship. I was with him two years and can vouch for him. He eagerly wants to be your friend."[10] The gift could be used for both old and new chess.

The King looked at it a while and bade that he

who sent such a gift be thanked for it and he added, "In return for this, we shall surely be friends." A short time later Bard had the white bear led into the hall before the King. The King's men greatly admired the beast.

Bard said, "Lord, this bear was sent to you by Gunnar, from Greenland."

The King said, "Great are the gifts of this man, but what does he want in return for it?"

Bard answered, "It appears, lord, that he wants your friendship and wise counsel."

"Why should he not have them both?" said the King.

One day after winter had passed, Bard asked the king to go into the main hall. He did so, and when they got there, Bard brought in before the King the walrus skull in all its shining glitter.

He said, "The noblest of men, Gunnar of Greenland, sent you this treasure." The King looked over the skull carefully. He thought it was most worthy and he bade his men safeguard it.

Then he said, "Tell me now, Bard, what's behind these gifts. I know more is at the bottom of all this than friendship alone."

Bard said, "It is as I told you, lord. He wishes to have your friendship and wise counsel in the matter of catching a fox, one who has brought great shame on Greenland."

The King asked what fox that might be.

Bard said, "He is an Icelander who slew a father and four sons in a single night. He has since sailed into the wilderness with six men and built a house out of great beams. We found him and set fire to the building, but water ran out of the building everywhere and put out the fire. The water sprang out of the top of the building as well as the bottom and middle, but nowhere did we see a source for this water."

The King said, "Is this the same fox who built

a trading ship in Iceland but who had never before seen a trading ship, who sailed to Greenland in this ship, and when he had been there some years had a great slander stirred up about him, and who avenged himself so bravely that he singlehandedly killed five in one night?"

Bard said, "We are talking about one and the same."

The King asked what the lay of the land was like there. Bard told him exactly.

"The men are still there?" asked the King.

Bard said, "When we parted, he said no one would shamefully drive him out of there."

"That might be," said the King, "but it could happen that he may yet have more to say about that. Anyway, I advise you not to go there again, for if you do, you will not escape."

Bard said, "But I have so promised Gunnar, and that I cannot break."

They ended their talk, and the winter passed away.

Chapter 13--King Harald's Plan

In the spring Bard made ready his ship, and when that was done, he went to the King and said, "Lord, have you given some thought to Gunnar's need?"

The King said, "I have given some thought to your need -- that you need not go to Greenland, for you aren't bound in a feud with those men, having no wrong to repay them for. I have a feeling that harm will come to you if you go."

Bard said, "May you foretell the truth better in other things, lord."

The King said, "I think that if I'm wrong in this, then I indeed say little of truth. But if you must go, then I will give you some advice, since Gunnar and you set such store by it."

"I won't ignore it," said Bard.

"Then I guess," said the King, "that in the little valley that runs up to the glacier there must be water, and that Ref must have brought that water, by joining hollow logs together, under the walls of the building. There, I think, he joined two hollow beams to it, and the water runs from these into every part of the building. The whole building is made of hollow beams and each one opens into another so that from top to bottom the whole building is filled with water. In this way, I think, was the equipment meant to work. When it seemed to you that water was coming out from all over the building, but there wasn't a joint to be seen, I think he had bored long holes, so narrow they could only be closed with thin carved plugs, and these plugs he placed everywhere back in the building's beams. Yet these plugs, I think, are not fixed in the wood. He can easily take them out when he wants to, so that water can spurt out of the building. All these plugs, of course, have been set with his usual skill, and both the plugs and the beams have been cut from the same kind of wood. Now this is my advice for Gunnar, that he go north in the spring in two ships, twelve men in each. The first twelve must dig a ditch to the north of the building, as long as the building itself and deep enough to come to a man's shoulders. Thus, they will likely find the hollow logs carrying the water, and if such is the case, then they should there dam up the brook so no water can enter the building. The other twelve should set fire to the building, and it would then seem to me that the building should burn, since no water can get to it. Having said that, I will now promise Gunnar that either Ref will flee the building and Greenland, or he will take Gunnar. Still, it isn't clear to me how this man could ever escape this plan, unless he is the cleverest of men. But I don't want you yourself to go, Bard, for I don't know how you will fare with Ref.

Bard said it could not be otherwise and thanked the King for his advice. He then cast off the mooring lines.

Chapter 14--Bard and Gunnar Meet Ref Again

Now it is said that Ref stayed in the wilderness, and his sons by now had become the worthiest of men. That same spring he sent his sons south to the settlement to meet with those men, spoken of before in this saga, who had promised Ref their help.[11] The brothers went secretly, and Gunnar learned nothing of their journey.

Once these men knew of Ref's message, they were pleased and went right away to join him. Next, Ref had fitted out the ship he had brought from Iceland. He had kept it in the ship-shed, and it was tarred as tightly as a bucket. He had the ship loaded with Greenland wares, walrus hides and ivory, and animal furs.

Once the ship was ready, they sailed it north to that fjord nearest the one where Ref's building was and anchored the ship there in a little stream. Altogether, there were Helga, Ref's wife, and Thormod, her foster brother, Thormod, Ref's youngest son, and the twelve men who came from the settlement. Ref said that he and his other two sons would stay in the building for a while.

Bard's journey went very well, and he landed in Greenland just where he wanted to. Gunnar welcomed Bard joyfully. They set men to guard Bard's goods, then went at once into the wilderness with as many men as the King had told them. Since they now knew the way, they quickly got to that fjord in which Ref's building stood.

Gunnar beached his ship in the outer part of the fjord because it was too hard to row the ship loaded with all their stores. They thought it easier to walk into the fjord. Bard and his men rowed all the way to the building. Gunnar and his men met him there. They all went up to look at the building.

Nothing had changed, at least from what they could see, except that a ditch had been dug as wide as the sea side of the building, and it ran down to the beach. The water near the shore was deep now, for the tide was in, and this ditch was no deeper than a man's waist.

At this moment a man came around the corner of the building. They knew at once who he was. It was Ref. He welcomed them and asked for the news. Bard said he would say nothing.

"Other than the fact that in this building you are about to die, there is," Bard said, "little news!"

Right away Bard had the ditch dug, and in a little while they found logs wound round with birch bark. They chopped up the logs, and a great deal of water spurted out. Gunnar and his men dragged wood to the building and set fire to it. At first a lot of water ran out of the building, but soon it began to dry up.

At this point Ref went out of the building and asked who had given them this idea. Bard said it was none of his business.

Ref said, "I know for sure that unless a cleverer man had helped you, none of you would have figured this out."

Bard said, "However that may be, we are now masters of you and your goods, and we'll either hang you there where you stand so you can look over your farm, or you shall burn."

Ref spoke this verse:

A sword-bearer, well-tried
Thinks our scheme to have beat.
Such was not unlooked for.
I'll bet the ring-giver (man)
Eager for sword-sound,
A worse trick will find,
Before he catches me!
My will shall win.

Ref then turned back into the building.

They added more wood to the fire, and the blaze grew and made great steam. All of a sudden they heard a loud cracking sound come from the building, and to their great surprise, the side of the building which faced the sea fell down! It had been fixed so that it fell in the ditch at the edge of the beach.

The surface was now as flat as a board.

Then, just as the building fell, out from there came a ship on wheels, which rolled at once to the sea! Ref and his men then raised sail, and there was a breeze from the north on the fjord. Under the parts of the building which fell were four of Bard's men. They died at once.

Chapter 15--The Pursuit

Bard called out to his men, and the eight of them ran to the ship. They raised sail at once and rowed as hard as they could. Bard soon gained on Ref and his men.

Gunnar was searching the building, but he found nothing of value, so he turned back down the fjord with his men towards his ship.

Ref saw that Bard was gaining and he said, "First we must take in our sail. It seems to me they won't suspect we would really wait for them, and their ship is sailing so fast, they'll run alongside us before they can stop. When they do, Stein, you cut their stays. Bjorn, you start splashing with the oars, so it will seem to them we are trying hard to run, but in fact, you make our boat slow down."

Ref then cut the wheels off the ship, picked up a small spear, and sharpened it well.

It is said about Bard and his men that they kept on rowing under sail, for they didn't believe Ref would stop, and their ship soon ran up alongside Ref's ship. At that moment Ref threw the spear at Bard. It flew straight into him and pinned him to the ship's side. Stein then cut all their stays, and the sail went overboard with all the rigging, and it looked as if the boat would roll over. At this, Ref raised his sail, and they were soon very far away. Ref and his men then made their way out of the fjord. Bard's crew saved their rigging and made for shore under the headland.

Gunnar and his men saw Ref sailing out of the inner part of the fjord. He thought it strange that he had neither seen nor heard from Bard and his men. He bade his men hurry to the ship and sail towards the point where the fjord seemed to end. They did so, but by now the daylight had largely gone.

When Ref and his sons came out of the strait and the fjord opened up again, they saw Gunnar and his men rowing from land as fast as they could. By then it had begun to grow very dark, and there was little moonlight.

Ref said, "We must still row with the greatest vigor, but you, Bjorn, make our sail fall, little by little, until it's all the way down."

They did so, and after a while Gunnar said to his men, "You are rowing in the worst way! Before, we were so near them I thought we could quickly overtake them, but now they have drawn away from us so much that their ship looks like a tiny speck! There must be more wind there. We've failed, and had better now turn back to land so as not to be tossed on the high seas at night looking for Ref."

They did so.

In the morning Bard's men came to Gunnar and said everything had gone wrong. They had with them Bard's body. Gunnar turned back to the settlement and was less than pleased with his journey, and it was commonly said by men that few had ever been hurt worse by a single man.

Those who had been with Bard quickly sold the ship's wares and sailed to Norway in the autumn, carrying no treasure this time, from Gunnar to King Harald. They told the King of Bard's death and their dealings with Ref. The King thought his foreboding hadn't been far off.

Chapter 16--Ref Goes to Norway

Ref and his sons then went back to their ship

and made merry. They got it ready for sailing and once that was done, they put to sea. They had an easy but long voyage. They made Norway in the fall and landed on Aedey Island. The islanders asked who was the master of this ship. Ref said he was, that his name was Narfi, and that he was an Icelander. He asked where the King was. The islanders told him the King was in Trondheim. Narfi then sailed to the mainland. He anchored his ship in a hidden bay, left his men behind, and rented a six-oar boat and pilot. Only his sons and wife went with him. His men guarded the ship.

Not much is said of Narfi's trip before he got to the marketplace in Nidaros. There he rented a small house where they stayed a few nights. He told his sons to be most careful never to leave Helga alone in the house. He had a cowled blue cloak made for himself, and he always wore a walrus hide belt. He also tied a white beard on and acted like an old trader. He always dressed like this when he went about the market, and he carried a short spear with an iron-bound handle.

The King was in the town with a great many men. One of his men was Grani, called Sheath-Grani, a fair man, and much taken with fine weapons and clothes. Grani was much given to women and lovemaking, and for this reason he had angered many, but nothing was done about it, for Grani was close to the King.

So it went until one day when the King was to hold a large Thing in the town. It was widely made known to everyone. Narfi went to the Thing with his sons, Stein and Thormod. Bjorn stayed home with his mother, but, as he was more interested in what went on at the Thing, after a while he went there too. Narfi saw Bjorn, went over to him, and asked who was staying with Helga. Bjorn said no one was. Narfi went back to the house at once.

A little while after Bjorn left, a man came to the house. He was wearing blue clothes and seemed to make much of himself. Helga greeted this man and asked his name. He said his name was Grani, and that he was one of the King's men.

"I have come here for this," he said, "to buy myself a woman."

Helga told him to go elsewhere for that. Grani said it wasn't fitting that an old man should have a young woman, so fine and fair. She said she would make her own judgment about that. Grani said he wasn't a shy man and grabbed for her. She sprang up and defended herself, wrestling with him. At this moment Narfi came to the window and looked in. When Grani saw the window darken, he broke out of Helga's grasp and ran to the door. Narfi also wanted to get to the door, but Grani got there first and took to his heels. Then Helga ran to the door and tried to hold Narfi back.

"Let Grani go," she said, "for he has done you no harm."

Narfi pushed her aside and ran after Grani, urging him to stop. But Grani ran as fast as ever until he came to a woven wood fence. There was now only a short distance between them, and he saw then that he would be taken.

He turned around and said, "Think about what you are doing. If you slay me, it will be your death, and I shall do you no harm as long as you are here in town." He begged for mercy as best he could.

Narfi said, "It is true that you are ill-mannered in everything. You hold yourself better than other men. You think yourself a great man, yet you do only great shame, and you don't even know how you should act at a moment like this, you're so afraid. Make yourself ready. I shall not grant your request for quarter."

Grani had an ax in hand, and with it he parried the thrust. He did this several times, but Narfi did not let up on him, and it ended, finally, with Narfi's driving his spear through him. Narfi then dragged him up beside the fence while he was in his death struggle and hid him there., But suddenly it came into his mind that it wouldn't be wise to hide the body, and it would likely turn out better if he told the King himself. So, Narfi went first to the house and told Helga to get their goods to the ship and so order the pilot. Narfi then went back to the Thing.

There was a very great crowd of men about, and Narfi pressed through them until he got before the King. At this moment the King was speaking to the grievances of men, but Narfi began to speak anyway.

"Lord King," he said, "We, Sword Grani and I had a milk-agreement today, when he wanted to mountain-gorge my wife.[12] I large-casked him through the straw-bender's eye. Then long-housed I, lord. Then long-housed he, lord. Then nest-balled I him, lord, and he many-horsed against me. Then I fair-tufted him, and he ship-bearded then about. Then bush-bundled I him, lord, under a wood fence nearby, and finally, I cloth-worked over him."

Narfi turned away at once and hurried to his boat. During the evening and the night they went south along the shore until they reached it. They put to sea at once.

Chapter 17--Narfi's Message to King Harald

Now it is said of King Harald at the Thing, that while Narfi was making his announcement, the King didn't stop him, but no one felt he gave much heed to it either. When Narfi had finished, the King broke the silence and said, "Who is this man who just stood before us in a blue coat and great walrus hide belt, and where does he come from?"

Men said that they never did know where he came from, but that he had been in town for a few days, rented a small house, and called himself Narfi.

The King said, "What do you think he said?" They said they would never know, that it was only nonsense or madness.

"That may be so," said the King, "but he seemed to me to be a man of no little mark--and where is our man, Sheath-Grani? Call him before me."

They went off, but didn't find him.

At this point the King said, "Things are getting worse. The man started speaking this way: 'We, Sword House Grani and I, had a milk-agreement today. He wanted to mountain-gorge my wife.' This, I think, means that he would have dealt with my man Sheath-Grani, for the sheath is the house of the sword. He would have been among the houses looking for women, and it may have been that he ran across the wife of this Narfi. In Iceland there is a drink called 'misa,' but it is the same drink as milk, thus they must have had a 'misagreement.' He also said the man wanted to 'mountain-gorge' his wife, but the word for 'mountain-gorge' is like the word for seducing a woman, and thus he meant to take her. Then he said he 'large-casked' him through the 'straw-bender's eye.' That is clear enough. 'Large cask' is like another word for seeing, and you know that the wind is called 'straw-bender' and the wind's eye is another name for window. Thus he saw through the window those two together in the room. Then 'long-housed I, King,' he said, 'and long-housed he.' Now the word 'long-house' is like another word for running, thus both of them must have run. He must have quickly leaped over the outer fence when he saw the two together. That, Grani would have heard, and it may be that he then left off his business there and tried to save himself. 'Then I nest-balled him,' he said. He must have egged him to stop, for a 'nest-ball' is an egg. Then he 'many-horsed,' but many horses together is called a stand, thus he must have taken a stand against him. Then he said he 'fair-tufted' him, and the man 'ship-bearded.' Now there are good cloaks in Iceland that are shaggy or tufted, but the word 'tufted' is like a word for thrust, so that when he said he 'fair-tufted' him, he meant he had thrust through him. 'Ship-bearded,' he said. But another word for beard also means a ship's prow, thus the man will have struggled greatly in death.[13] 'Then bush-bundled I him under a fence nearby,' he said. A bush-bundle is a heavy load, and he must have carried him under the fence. Then he said he 'cloth-worked' over him. This is a phrase that weavers use in Iceland to mean they've finished a job off, thus he must have covered the man."

"Now I wish," said the King, "that you look for these men, both the slain and the slayer."

They did as the King ordered, and they found the dead Grani, but Narfi they didn't find.

In the morning the King called a meeting and said, "Yesterday we learned of something that were better if it happened less often -- the death of one of my men. I would not have thought this Icelander would dare to do this here in our midst. Now I shall guess who this man is. It is that same Ref who did such great wrongs to the Greenlanders."

Then the King called for men to search for Ref, both on land and at sea, and they did what he ordered.

Chapter 18--Ref Meets King Svein

Now it is said that Ref didn't stop sailing until he came to Denmark. There he went at once to find the King and told him all about why he had come there.[14] Ref asked to be allowed to stay. The King said there seemed to be, in his story, great need for his harsh deeds, and he added, "I think you and your sons can expect much help from me. Now, because you have sought us out, and also because you have brought here those wares not easy for us to get due to our enemies, walrus skins for our ships' rigging, I shall give you a home and land where it pleases me. Your sons, Stein and Bjorn, shall stay with us. Their honor, and the worth of this deal, shall be seen in the time that they are tried with us. But your son, Thormod, shall stay with you."

Ref said he would willingly accept all this, and he added, "But first, lord, we must look after our goods, and get the two brothers ready for their stay."

The King said so it should be.

Ref and his men went to his ship. It so happened that they had in there Greenland wares, walrus tusks, and other pelts, and many other things seldom seen in Denmark. They had five white bears and fifty falcons, fifteen of them white.[15]

Chapter 19--Ref is Outlawed

It so happened that in the autumn the ship that once belonged to Bard came back from Greenland to Norway. King Harald asked about Bard's death and all that had gone on there. One day the King called a meeting and told everyone about the slaying of his man, Bard, in Greenland.

"I know for sure now," he said, "all of what happened in Grani's slaying. Narfi was Ref Steinson. I shall give him a nickname, and call him Clever Ref. Now, though he is a very able man, we must still guard our honor, to make others loath to kill my men, and for this do we here today outlaw this man from all Norway, so far as our power reaches."

After that, the King told Erik, Grani's brother, to take sixty men south with him to Denmark to seek Ref's life.

Chapter 20--Erik's Pursuit of Ref

Erik and his men made ready for their voyage. They didn't stop until they got to Denmark, and after a few days they anchored in a good harbor in Jutland. When they got there, an old, gray-haired man came up. He wore a wretched cowled cloak, carried two crutches, and had a white beard. They gave him a good welcome and asked his name. The man called himself Sigtrygg. They asked where his family were from. He said they were once Norwegian, but now had been in Denmark a while, and were very poor. They said he seemed like a good man and could tell them much. He asked what they wanted to know. They said they wanted to know about a man called Ref who would have come to Jutland that summer with a ship and some men.

Sigtrygg said, "If I tell you what you want to know, is there anything in it for me?"

They said he wouldn't lack food for a while.

Sigtrygg said, "I won't tell you about Ref just for food, for I know from men's talk that you are seeking his life. These are the terms under which I will take you to Ref and his sons and the twelve men who came with him in the summer. I must get an ounce of silver from each of you, and a costly gift from your ship. You must agree to take me to Norway, if I wish, at your own cost, and you must put me in charge of this journey, until we find Ref."

They agreed to this.

Sigtrygg said, "Now we must strike this ship tent at once and row around the headland."[16]

They did so, and landed the ship again.

"Now I shall go up," said the old man, "and two of you come with me, and we'll find out what we can about Ref."

They did so. There was a woods nearby, and when they had gone a little way into the woods, armed men jumped them -- Ref's sons and the other twelve.

The Norwegians were both seized. Sigtrygg cast off his rags, and also his beard. Then they all went to the sea by another way. There lay two longships and two hundred men. King Svein had sent these to Ref, once he found out that men had been sent to look for him. Ref and his men got weapons and they all rowed off to attack Erik and his men. When they met, it was over quickly. All but ten of Erik's men were killed, and those ten were all captured.

At this point Ref said, "Now it so happens, Erik, that here is Sigtrygg, your partner and customer, whom you paid off last night. I have done what I promised. Here you see Ref and his sons. Now, because I have slain your brother, I will spare your life -- if you will swear never again to seek my life or my sons'. You must also tell King Harald the whole truth of this business, and tell him also that I have rewarded him for that plotting against me when he helped those men who wanted to have my life. King Harald shall not be fated to cause my death, for there is against him in Denmark one more dangerous than I, and one who can destroy more."[17]

Erik then swore the oath, and after that Ref got them a twelve-oar boat and all the things Erik and his men would need for the journey.

Ref took their longship and brought it to King Svein. The King greatly praised what Ref had done and said his deeds were both brave and manly.

He added, "You shall keep the name Sigtrygg here in our kingdom, because it is seldom used here, and at this name-giving we wish you to have this gold ring. It weighs a mark. Also, you must accept from us twelve farms west in Vendil, of your own choice, for I believe you are a very wise man."

Ref thanked the King well for these princely gifts and all the honor which he had shown him. Ref then went to the farms he had been given with Helga, his wife, and Thormod, their son. There Sigtrygg became the greatest of men, and when he had lived there some years, he left on a journey to Rome, to seek the home of the holy apostle Peter, but on this voyage he became sick and died. He was richly buried at a monastery in Frakkland.[18]

Stein and Bjorn were with King Svein a long time, and he valued them so greatly he got noble marriages for them in Denmark. They both settled there and were thought to be the best of men. From Stein has come Archbiship Absalom, who lived in the days of King Valdimar Knutson. Ref's son Thormod left for Iceland after the fall of King Harald and took up land in Kvennabrek. He married in Iceland, and many of the best men have come from him.

We end there the saga of Clever Ref.

Notes on The Saga of Clever Ref

[1]King Hakon the Good ruled Norway from 934-961.

[2]The name means "fox" in Old Icelandic.

[3]Good, hard cutting weapons were often fashioned with a steeled edge. Cutting weapons without this edge, made all of one piece of iron, were of lesser quality and softer.

[4]In this type of building there were two wings; one for women, one for men.

[5]There were two settlements in Greenland, one on the southern tip called Brattahlid or the East Settlement, and one further north on the west coast called the West Settlement. It would appear that Ref is here referring to the East Settlement.

[6]A serious insult, for which a man could be killed on the spot without penalty, according to the ancient laws (Grágas II, 147).

[7]The period from the middle of August to the middle of September.

[8]Harald Sigurdson (Hard-Ruler) ruled Norway from 1042-1066.

[9]The western British Isles.

[10]The older game differed from the true chess primarily in that there was only one King, attacked by the white pieces and defended by the black.

[11]The spring Bard left Harald.

[12]This and what follows is a sequence of puns which do not lend themselves well to translation. The message is explained by the King in the subsequent chapter. It is a clever way for Ref to announce the slaying, which he must do, and still provide enough time for escape.

[13]Apparently referring to the motion of a

ship's prow in heavy seas.

[14]Svein Ulfson ruled Denmark from 1047-76. A large part of his reign was marked by conflict with Harald of Norway.

[15]White falcons were the most highly prized.

[16]The ship tent was a board shelter which came down when the ship was underway.

[17]A reference to King Svein.

[18]The land of the Franks, modern France.

THE STORY OF THORSTEIN OF THE EAST FJORDS

There was once a quick young man named Thorstein from the East Fjords of Iceland who wanted to make a pilgrimage to Rome. He sailed first to Denmark. At that time, King Magnus the Good was in Denmark, constantly fighting great battles.[1]

One day it happened, as Thorstein walked along, that he saw a man making a stand under an oak tree while four men attacked him. This man defended himself very well indeed, and it seemed to Thorstein that he had a very strong spirit.

Thorstein then said to himself, "Is it not braver to help the one who fights alone than the four who are against him?" Whereupon he drew his sword and went over. He swung it strongly and often and slew three of the men in a short time. The man who fought in front of the tree slew the fourth.

This man was young, and he wore a silk jacket over a coat of mail. He was a handsome man, but greatly tired from the fight. Thorstein said to him, "What is the name of the man I have helped?"

The man answered, "Styrbjorn is my name. I am one of King Magnus's men. Things were looking pretty dim for me before you came. My own men had scattered into the woods. You've been such a great help to me that it's now hard to reward you justly. What are you planning to do?"

Thorstein said, "I'm an Icelander and I mean to go south to Rome."

Strybjorn said, "Would you put off this southern trip and stay here?"

Thorstein answered, "Maybe, but if I were to do that, it would only be to serve King Magnus or one of his men.

Styrbjorn said, "Do you like King Magnus?"

"Indeed I do," said Thorstein, "for he is a noble chieftain and famous in all lands."

Styrbjorn said, "I think it's wise you go on with your journey, for it is a pressing one, but visit me when you come back. I am always with King Magnus's men."

Then they parted, and Thorstein went on to Rome.

He came back from the south in the spring, and arrived just as King Magnus began a feast. He went to the hall and asked to go in. The doorkeeper answered and said it wasn't customary for unknown men to enter while the King was feasting.

Thorstein said, "Ask the man called Styrbjorn to come out."

At this another man at the door ran inside, calling out with laughter, "Styrbjorn must go outside!" Soon all the men had sprung up, and one said, "Go outside now, Styrbjorn--when an Icelander calls you! He sure thinks he knows the names of the King's men, but we know no one here by that name!" Whereupon, from this seat, each man took to great ridicule and mockery and said, "Styrbjorn must go outside!"

Then the King began to speak. He said, "This is an unworthy sport. A man could have more than one name. You shall not mock this name any longer."

And so it came to be as the King wished.

Soon the King rose from his seat and went outside. He was wearing a beautiful cloak. He said, "Welcome Icelander. Put this cloak over you and go inside. A bath shall be drawn for you. You are welcome among the King's men. None shall be so bold as to do you any harm."

All were astonished at this.

Later on, when he was with the King's men, Thorstein became glum and fell silent. The King said to him then, "Now who do you think our Styrbjorn might be?"

Thorstein answered, "I most hope that is what you call yourself."

The King said, "You are right, and as my rescuer you must be well-rewarded." Then the King began the whole story and told it all from the start when they had met in Denmark.

Sometime later, they journeyed up along the land to the north. Once, while at anchor in a harbor, some were on land preparing food. They made porridge, and when the great bowl came to Thorstein, he ate all of it! The King's men laughed at this and said, "Icelander, you sure know how to eat porridge!"

The King smiled and spoke this verse:

Alone the great fighter
Made three fall
Together in battle.
He outdid them.
But ate the great eater,
On a Northland voyage,
Porridge for three.
He outdid them!

"This very man," said the King, "gave me great help when you were nowhere around, and he did so when he knew not who I was. For that, he is a truly noble man. It is thus not wise to mock an unknown man, for it would take a long search to find a braver or more friendly man. To some, it would even seem good luck to find such a man."

Thorstein said then, "It's clear, lord, that God sent me to defend you. Your bearing struck me as unlike that of any common man, and thus I chose to help you."

The King treated Thorstein well, and one day he said to him, "How do things stand with you? What would you most like to do? Would you like to stay here and take a wife?"

Thorstein answered, "That is a noble offer, and

no doubt, while you live my honor would be greatest here. But a long life is promised to no one, and if I lost your protection, I should then get enemies. And yet, I know for sure that you would provide for me so that I would enjoy your generosity for a long time."

The King said, "That was wisely said."

He then provided Thorstein with much money for his trip back to Iceland. Thorstein settled in Iceland, and was thought to be the luckiest of men.

There is no more of him to tell.

Note on The Story of Thorstein of the East Fjords

[1]Probably during the years 1042-1047, which saw Magnus's attempts to subjugate Svein Ulfson, who also claimed the Danish throne.

THE SAGA OF VALLA LJOT

Chapter 1--Halli and Torfi

Sigurd was the son of Karl the Red. He married the daughter of Ingjald of Gnupufell and had three sons. The oldest was named Hrolf; the others were Halli and Bodvar. All were big men and strong. Hrolf was a troublemaker and very greedy. Halli had a ready wit and was skilled at law, but he was the most arrogant of all. Bodvar was a good-natured man and he became a sea-trader.

Sigurd took sick. He called his sons around him and told them always to stick together. He said he knew their natures well and he told them, "Don't be small-minded, but be careful of your honor." After this he died. At that time Hrolf was eighteen years old, Halli fourteen, and Bodvar twelve.

Torfi was a rich but low-born man who lived in Modruvale at Torfufell. At this time the chieftain Eyjolf lived at Modruvale, and his son Gudmund lived with him.[1] Torfi's wife died, and after his wife's death he was kind to Sigurd's sons. Later on, Torfi went to their home and called them all together.

He told them, "There's been a long, close friendship between us, and for my part I wish to further it. So now I want to talk to your mother and propose to her. Though we are unequal in birth, yet through my money and talent, we'll both profit from the match."

Hrolf said to go ahead and ask his mother about the matter. He did so, and she answered, " In this matter I will follow my sons' wishes, and if it seems to them an equal match, I won't oppose it."

Torfi said, "What do you think, Halli?"

He answered, "This matter belongs more properly to Hrolf, the oldest brother. He has greater foresight in such things."

Torfi then asked Hrolf and Bodvar together about the match, and they said it was not at all unpromising and that it should take place that fall.

Then Halli said, "I wanted to wait for your advice though I expected you to say what you did. I can't see the wisdom of it. Such a man would not make an equal match, and very little honor would come from it. I can't agree that giving my noble mother to a freedman is an honorable marriage."[2]

Hrolf said it didn't seem that way to him. His mother said she wouldn't be guided by Halli, and she added, "I consent to this match."

Halli said it would be as she wished. The wedding feast was fixed for the beginning of winter.[3]

One day later on when Halli came into his mother's bedroom, she said to him, "Today I have to pay our housewomen's wages. I'm sending you to Torfufell to tell Torfi to send me a pig. He will give it up if he knows I need it, and though the pig will be hard to handle, don't you be too hot-headed."

Halli said, "I'll go, for he is a faithful friend of yours."

When Halli got there, Torfi was at work and didn't look up at him.

Halli said to Torfi, "My mother sent me here to ask you to send her a pig to feed her women."

Torfi still didn't look at him, but he said, "That I can do. Catch it yourself."

Halli answered, "It isn't noble to run around in the filth of an old sow like a common man."

Torfi answered, "What says the fearless lord?"

"Send in there anyone you want," said Halli, "but I'll not risk it."

Then Torfi said, "I guess you don't consider yourself as brave as the pig!"

Halli answered by saying, "It would be better if that hadn't been said. I do not equate my valor with that of the pig. That can be called a taunting insult.[4]

Halli then leaped to the gate and flung it open. He quickly cut off the pig's head and took the animal outside with him.

Torfi said, "Now take it back and give it to your mother."

Halli didn't answer, but rode away on the path to his home.

There were many woods in the district, and soon Halli jumped off his horse and waited in the forest until he saw a man in a blue cloak riding across the river. He saw that it was Torfi. Halli had both spear and sword. He jumped up, leaped straight at Torfi, and struck him his deathblow. Halli then hid the body under the riverbank, but took the horse with him. He came home and greeted his mother. She asked about his errand, and he said that when he had last seen Torfi it was clear that no matter what was agreed on before, Torfi was not now coming to her bed, nor was he sending her any pig.

He told her, "Though you may not believe this, your marriage is not likely to happen."

She answered,"I think you often go after trouble, and this will be the beginning of your bad luck. The men around here, Eyjolf's men, will take up suits against you, and you'll either be outlawed or slain."

Halli said, "You don't have to scold me so much for this because Torfi's life was of little value, though he may have seemed worthy to you."

"You may be right," she answered, "but it would have been better if this hadn't happened."

Later he journeyed to Gnupufell to see his kinsman, Ingjald, and told him what happened. Ingjald answered, "You must go to your kinsman and close friends in Svarfadale. What did you charge him with?"

Halli said, "He insulted me because I didn't want him to marry my mother and so dishonor our family. Now my life is in danger, and I don't know what will happen--at best a narrow escape in a lawsuit. Still, he called me more cowardly than a pig!"

"That was a bad insult," answered Ingjald, "stay with us now, until your suit is ended."

Later, Halli went to find his kinsman, Viga-Glum, who lived at Thvera River, and they went together to see Eyjolf and offer him a settlement for his Thingman, Thorfi. They said, "We wish to honor you in this so we'll pay a hundred ounces of silver[5] for the death of Torfi and we'll also drop our suit against him for insulting Halli. It's unlikely that any more can be gotten from our kinsmen so we shouldn't let this make trouble."

Eyjolf answered, "It shall be so. Halli is bound to us in kinship and he is indeed high-born."

They settled on these terms. Halli was seventeen years old when this settlement was made.

Chapter 2--Halli Moves Away

Bodvar went to seek his fortune, but Hrolf the Greedy stayed home and kept up the family farm. Bodvar was abroad a long time and he became a worthy and esteemed sea-trader in the twelve years of his journeys. Halli started his own farm and married Signy, Bersi's daughter, and a kinswoman of the Modruvellings, so things went well between Halli and Eyjolf. Halli said that the marriage bonds were the surest way of becoming friends. Eyjolf said he had seen that rightly. Halli handled a great many suits for Eyjolf.

Later on Eyjolf drowned in the Gnupufell River. He had been prime-signed before he was buried in the yard of his house.[6] After that his son, Gudmund the Mighty, took over. Things went well between Halli and Gudmund. He backed Halli with his own men, and Halli received great honor from Gudmund because he was a stone-breaker[7] in Gudmund's suits, and for this he was called Feuding Halli. At this point in the saga, Halli was forty years old, but he was still unequal to Gudmund in power or wealth. Halli's son was named Bersi, and he was a promising young man. Hrolf was a rich man now, but still spiteful.

It is said that one time Gudmund invited a lot of men to a feast in Modruvale. Halli was there as usual. There was talk about many things, and at one point Halli said, "Leadership seems very strange in Iceland when the best men here in the north are leaving, especially from this district."

Gudmund answered, "It's often said that I am eager for honor, but still, I wouldn't want to be a chieftain anywhere else but here."

Halli said, "Still, Gudmund, though the number of good men is greater now in this district, there are others not far behind."

Gudmund asked, "Which ones are they?"

Halli said, "One is Svarfadale."

Gudmund answered, "You should speak with more truth and wisdom. It snows all the time there and the winters are very harsh."

Halli said, "Yet it usually happens with such outlying valleys that more people will go there to buy meat than will come here, and thus more money will be made there."

Gudmund answered, "I still don't see why you praise this district. It doesn't seem worthy to me."

Halli said, "I've been thinking of changing the way I now must live, and I want to move my farm there."

Gudmund said, "Why is it better for you to live there than here?"

Halli said, "My high-born kinsman have settled there and that's why I want to go. Here I am your stone-breaker, and that happens to make me little liked. Also, there are some men over me in this district, but that won't be the case if I leave. Anyway, we can still be friends. I should also say openly now that much hatred came from my dealings with Einar, your brother, and I want to get away from that."[8]

"That is somewhat true," said Gudmund, "but I suspect that was less a matter of honor than of your unpopularity."

Halli answered, "Nor is it a lesser reason that my kinsmen, the sons of Ingjald, are over me here, and I can't be the greatest of our kinsmen while we're all here together. But there I can be the mightiest."

Gudmund said, "I don't think you'll get more honor there than you had here. I know of four men there who won't move over for you."

Halli answered, "Who are these four who will stand against me?"

Gudmund replied, "The first is the mightiest man in the valley, Valla Ljot, son of the chieftain Ljotolf. Next, there is Thorgrim, his brother, The third is Bjorn, of Hofsa River, and the fourth is Thorvard, his brother. Those two are Thorgrim's sons, both high-born men. I don't think you should go up there to your kinsman, Thorir. It seems to me you'd have to fight a stronger force."

Halli answered, "I mean to go anyway."

Later, Halli journeyed to see Thorir Vemundarson and tell him what he wanted to do. He said he wanted to buy land and asked Thorir where there was land for sale. Thorir said to him, "I know of land for sale in Klaufabrekka. There's a little grassland there, and I'll get some of it for you. If you must move your home there, I'll buy that land for you, but I think it would be wise to be quiet about it. Stubborn and high-minded men here would be angered by it."

Halli said he wasn't going to be driven out and told Thorir to buy the land. A while later he moved his home there, but asked leave of no one to settle.[9] The Svarfadalers paid little heed to this since Ljot was their chieftain and they quickly agreed with him--among them, he alone ruled.

Ljot was a very big man, cheerful, and not given to meddling in other men's business. By this one will know what pleased him: He had two pieces of battle gear, a short blue coat and a spear-ax with an iron-bound handle. He always carried these when the war mood came over him, and he was very happy when he wore the dark coat and gripped the battle ax in his hand.

Chapter 3--Halli's Challenge

Hrolf was a landholder who lived above Klaufabrekka.[10] He was a high-born man. Thord and Thorvald were his sons. He took sick and died. The brothers inherited the homestead from their father and they asked Ljot to divide it up between them, both land and goods. Ljot couldn't go for a while, and it was Michaelmass when the meeting was finally held.[11] At this time Christianity was new in the land, and the keeping of holy days had just been brought into the laws.

Thorir and Halli went out and found the meeting. Snow had fallen on the landmarkers when Ljot began to divide the brothers' land. He divided the land by taking a straight line from a certain stone down to the river where he put up a sodmarker and said, "This is how I divide the land." This pleased the brothers well and everybody else too--except Halli.

Ljot said, "We haven't any business together here, Halli, but you are a clever man--does the division please you?"

Halli answered, "I think the land has been divided equally, but since you ask, I think the law was tampered with when you did this, and I can certainly say somrthing about that. Are you very skilled at law, Ljot?"

He said, "I don't know the law well."

Halli answered, "I think it's against the law to do this on Michaelmass, even though it's not a Sunday, and I'm going to charge you with a breech of sanctity."

Ljot answered, "This faith is young in the land."

Halli said, "According to the law a breech of sanctity has happened, and it isn't good for the lesser men here to see chieftains doing this."

Ljot answered that he had not done well and said, "It shall not happen again."

Halli said, "I have little more to say. Pay me a half-hundred of silver or I'll summon you."

Ljot answered, "It would be wiser if you don't summon me, and I'm not going to pay you for my lack of foresight. I think it would be best for you to quiet down and let me handle the matter."

Halli answered, "It benefits neither of us to forget this."

Ljot said, "You must have your right to demand a penalty, as is usual in such cases, but come to some agreement with me now and you'll get my thanks."

Halli answered, "It can't be that way--either pay up the money or I'll summon you."

Ljot said, "I don't want you to summon me. I would rather pay the money--and get friendship in return. Long have our kinsmen quarrelled among themselves. Maybe I am too much like them. I'll pay the money now since I don't want to anger the angel.[12] If your friendship is sincere, you have my trust. If you are doing this out of greed, or to challenge me--as I rather think--well, then that will yet come to light."

Halli took the money.

That same autumn there was a feast at Modruvale and Halli went to it. Bersi, his son, had some back to Iceland and was there also. Gudmund seated Halli nearest himself. He had heard about the matter between Halli and Ljot and he asked Halli, "How do you like it out in the valley?"

Halli said he liked it well enough.

Gudmund said, "Do the men support you out there?'

Halli answered that they seemed to.

"I have heard," said Gudmund, "that you demanded money from Ljot for a small offense of his."

Halli answered, "That's not quite right. I took up the matter so justice would be done, but he chose to do only what served him better. You can see here the silver."

"Yes," said Gudmund, "I see that you think you've done well, but something tells me there will be bloody heads before the start of winter. I don't think it's wise for you to stay there. I can buy land for you here, but I can't take care of you there."

Halli answered, "That's a good offer, but it's lacking in some ways, and because of that I won't leave. I want to try it out still longer in Svarfadale."

A while later, at Yule, Halli and Bersi went back to the valley.

Thorir asked Halli to a Yule feast at Grund--there was a church at the farm--but Bersi, Halli's sons, stayed home. Thorir sent men out after hay because there was a shortage of hay during Yule. Word of Halli's very unfriendly talk about their dealings came to the ears of Valla Ljot. After the feast, Halli made ready to leave, and that morning the shepherds from Grund and Vale met and gosssiped. They asked each other who had been the wittiest storyteller, but each man sided with his landholder. Then one of Thorir's men said there was more fun because Halli was there, and there's no better story-teller than Halli. At this point one of Ljot's housemen asked when Halli was leaving. A houseman of Thorir's said Halli would go on the last day of the feast. When the houseman came home, Thorir asked him who he had talked to. The man told him. Thorir then asked what they talked about, and the man told him what had been said.

"For sure," said Thorir, "it's clear, Halli, that you must go nowhere today."

He then told Halli what had happened and also what the housemen had talked about. He added, "It may mean nothing that they talk about your trip home, but I have a feeling it will go as Gudmund said--that Ljot would get the better of you in this matter."

Halli answered, "But what's between Ljot and me except good will?"

Thorir said, "He has misgivings about your case."

"I'm going anyway," said Halli.

Thorir answered, "Then my thirteen housemen shall follow you, but I feel sick, and so had better not go with them."

Halli said he didn't need them.

Chapter 4---Ljot's Answer

When they left they went up towards Hordabrekka. After a while, Halli said to the men, "Go back now. I'm too close to home for anyone to ambush us."

They did as Halli said.

Halli's sheep pen was close by the path, and Halli's houseboy cried out, "Men are there!"

Halli answered, "That might be my son, Bersi."

The houseboy said, "Those aren't our men. There are twelve of them, and one is wearing a blue cloak and has a spear-ax in his hand!"

"You go find Bersi," said Halli, and tell him that Ljot seems to want to iron out some details with me. There's no need for you to stay here."

He took off at once, in great haste.

Halli was wearing pants with the stockings attached, and he had a big cape over him which he threw off. He had a helmet on his head, a spiked pole in his hand, and a sword at his belt--and he bolted, riding right by them.

Ljot said to his men, "Don't hold off any longer. Take him now!"

They rode after him, but he turned around and came past them again, going downhill, and they couldn't catch him when they rode uphill either. Finally, Halli stopped on a little plain, and Ljot said, "See how he vaunts himself against us, standing higher than we are."

Halli answered, "I shall use my strength and swiftness. I won't stand and wait."

Ljot said, "Karl, your grandfather, would have stood even in his old age. He never would have let himself be chased like a goat."

Halli answered, "I'll make my stand here--if we fight alone. There's honor for you in that, but in this ambush, only shame."

Ljot answered, "That needs no saying. It shall be as you say."

Halli asked, "What do charge me with?"

Ljot answered, "The charge is this, that you shall no longer accuse me of not keeping holy days. Now if you meant well in this matter, and the chief angel Michael wants to give you victory, then you'll be helped in this fight. But if you acted from greed or to challenge me, then you have a lesser right to win and when he decides our case, you'll really enjoy that half-hundred you got from me!"

Ljot came at him with an iron-mounted shield. Halli swung at Ljot, and the blow was so hard that his sword stuck fast in the boss of the shield. Ljot then twisted the shield so fast that the sword broke at the handle, whereupon Ljot struck Halli his death-blow.

They carried him to the sheep pen and then went home to the farm and told everyone about it. Ljot made it known that he had slain Halli. Bersi went at once to Gudmund and told him what happened. Gudmund said he wasn't surprised. Bersi said he wanted to leave Iceland. At this time all duels and duelling law were forbidden.[13]

Chapter 5--Hrolf Breaks the Settlement

Gudmund took up the case and made ready to go to the Althing with a great many people. Ljot's kinsmen sought a settlement. Ljot had a large body of men with him and he had the backing of many chieftains, so by the strength of his kinsmen and the might of his friends, a settlement was made of a hundred ounces of silver for Halli's slaying.

That half-hundred which Ljot had paid Halli was not returned because Ljot wanted that to be payment for his lack of foresight. His friends wanted him to take back that half-hundred, but he wouldn't do it, saying it was too little a settlement for Halli's challenge. Gudmund wasn't happy with the way the case ended, but he safeguarded the money for Halli's kinsmen.

During the summer a ship from the mainland landed at Eyjafirth,[14] where a big market was set up. Several of the Svarfadalers set out for this place. Among them was one of the Thorgrimsons, Ljot's nephew, and his houseman. They carried wares. There was also a man named Sigmund. These Svarfadalers were sleeping in a little dale when in the light of dawn a man came to them and said, "You should know that the Eyjafirthers[15] are on the other side of the river mouth, and I've come to tell you to beware of them for they're not to be trusted. Come with me,

Thorvard, and I'll tell you more."

Thorvard answered, "I don't need your advice because I think you're not to be trusted."

But Thorvard left his tent and went with the man to a hill nearby where they talked about the matter. Then nine men came towards them, all dressed in black. Thorvard wanted to turn back, but the man who had tricked him dragged him into their midst. They attacked him at once and killed him. Sigmund pledged to avenge him. This treacherous deed was done by Hrolf the Greedy.

When Gudmund found Hrolf, he said he had been wrong not to abide by the settlement. He said it would come to no good. Hrolf said he hadn't been present at the settlement. Ljot took up the suit for the slaying of his kinsman, Thorvard. Gudmund sent word to Ljot that he wanted to settle the suit. He said to Ljot,"I want you to be fully honored by the settlement," and he said this business little pleased him and that those serve the district best who keep men from doing such harm.

To the Thing came the friends of both Gudmund and Ljot. They sought a settlement, and through the efforts of many others finally chose Skapti Thorodson, a friend of Ljot's, as a peacemaeker. Ljot said he himself wouldn't be stubborn, but that such a crime stirs up evil, since for many it's easier to kill the second time than the first. He also said that he would rather be attacked again than offend anyone.

Thorvard's death was paid off with two hundred ounces of silver. Hrolf was happier now than before, and he stayed that way for two years.

Chapter 6--Bjorn Seeks Revenge

A ship came out to Iceland during the summer and on it were Bodvar Sigurdson and Bersi Hallason. They quickly went to meet Gudmund. He told them what had been done and where the matter now stood. Bodvar was even-tempered and very calm about it. He said he was very pleased with Gudmund's foresight, and he hated all the quarrelling in the district. He said he would again go abroad and not get wound up in the matter.

During the winter, when Gudmund wasn't home, men from Kviabekk came out from Olafsfjord to buy goods. Asmund, their leader, bought some six hundred silver ounces worth of goods and said it would all be paid back. Bodvar said he wished Gudmund were there to vouch for them.

Asmund said, "It's well-known that we pay our debts."

Bodvar answered, "But I wish you'd bring the money here."

But Asmund said he wanted to take the goods back to Olafsfjord and pay for them when they were sold. Bodvar agreed, and afterwards they went away. Gudmund came home, and they told him about the deal.

He answered, "This deal wouldn't have happened if I had been there!"[16]

Soon Yule passed and the weather got better. Bodvar and Bersi asked to go claim payment for the goods, but Gudmund said it wouldn't be wise to go into the hands of the Svarfadalers, adding, "Although I think Ljot wouldn't allow an attack on you."

They went anyway, in a group of four, and when they reached Olafsfjord, their payment wasn't ready. Many had bought the goods, but Bodvar could collect the money only from Asmund. Bodvar and Bersi had come out there on a ferry owned by some Norwegians, but they stayed too long and a great frost came so they couldn't leave by ship. Asmund told them they were free to stay there with him. Bodvar accepted, and they were storm-bound for two weeks.

Later, a dry frost improved the road, but the fjord was still covered with ice, so they couldn't go by ship, and Asmund said, "You are more than welcome to stay with us longer, Bodvar."

Bodvar said that was a good offer, but he added, "We would rather get a guide and go overland."

Asmund said he didn't like the idea, but added, "I wish you good luck in parting."

"It must be this way," said Bodvar.

The twelve of them then rode on the heath until the road forked. Then the weather worsened and it began to snow. Soon the snow covered the path and the going was slow and unfamiliar for Bodvar, but he meant to cross Svarfadale during the night and reach Narfi's. Then night fell, and they could no longer see where they were going. At this point Bodvar said, "We've lost the path, and it's not going to get any lighter."

But they didn't stop until they stumbled on a house in the darkness. Men were sitting inside around the fire, and Bodvar knocked at the door. One of them went to the door and asked who was there.

Bodvar answered, "Who lives here, and what's this farm called?"

"Thorgrim Ljotolfson lives here,"[17] said the man, "and the farm is called Upsir. The cwner wants you to come in because it's harsh outside. He told me to tell you this, whoever you are."

Bodvar answered, "We don't want to go in unless the owner himself asks us."

The man went in and told Thorgrim that the men who had come wanted him to ask them in and he added, "They're very proud."

Thorgrim went outside, told them to lodge there for the night and asked who they were. Bodvar said some were Icelanders and some Norwegians, and he told his own name. Thorgrim went in before them and told them to sit down and be at home, and he added, "I won't take back this offer." He said no one would be more welcome, though no one was less expected, and he had a fire built for them.

Sigmund was there at the house (he was named before in this saga). He was the foster brother of the son of Thorgerd, Ljotolf's daughter. He was greatly startled and secretly reminded Thorgrim about what happened to Thorvard, his kinsman.

Thorgrim said he wasn't going to take up that case and added, "I want to treat them well who wish me no evil, and I should not want to betray those who have sought out my house."

They stayed there during the night. Thorgrim bolted the door and told them no one was to open it unless he said so.

He said, "He who disobeys me in this shall find trouble."

Sigmund didn't challenge this, and they all slept fast. But, there was a way out of the house through the barn, and so Sigmund got out.

There was a break in the weather, and it stopped snowing. Sigmund got snowshoes and went in the dark to see Bjorn at Hofsa River.[18] He woke him up, and Bjorn asked who had come. Sigmund told him. Bjorn asked why he was so excited.

Sigmund said there was a need for revenge and added, "You can now avenge your brother!"

"Who has come?" said Bjorn.

He answered, "Bodvar, Halli's brother, and he means to go south along the Eyjafjord shore."[19]

Bjorn said, "It doesn't seem right to kindle up feuds again just to settle this matter. The man is guiltless and has never been a part of the quarrels here in the land. It would be much more fitting if he were Hrolf; yet, even then it wouldn't be right. I also know the zeal of Thorgrim's kinsmen, and if harm is brought to their guests, they would find it very shameful."

Sigmund answered, "It's no great justice if they are killed, yet it's also a great pity if such a rascal as you still lives. It will often haunt us that your brother was slain in peace before us -- and now you won't avenge him!"

Bjorn got eight of his men together and said he wanted to see his kinsman, Ljot. He couldn't stand Sigmund's scolding. They went to Vale. Ljot asked what Bjorn wanted, to be riding so in the middle of the night.

Bjorn answered, "I mean to go and avenge Thorvard, my kinsman."

Ljot said, "Has Hrolf come?"

"No," said Bjorn, "but his brother Bodvar, has come to the valley."

Ljot said, "Is this your plan, kinsman, to slay a guiltless man and break the peace? I'll not go on this journey. I would hardly be honored for attacking my own brother in his home!"

Bjorn said, "We needn't attack your brother to get at them. We'll wait nearby for them to leave."

Sigmund said, "We can see when they leave."

Ljot said he wouldn't go.

They went away, and later Sigmund said, "Let's go to Tjarn for Thorstein and his son Eyjolf." They were hardy men and very brave.

When they got there, Bjorn said, "I need your help so our enemies won't go about this valley in peace." Thorstein agreed it must be done and rode with them in this undertaking, but Eyjolf, his son, had gone up to Saudadale.

Chapter 7--The Ambush

Meanwhile, Bodvar and his companions got ready to leave in the morning, and Thorgrim said, "I don't think you should use the main road, Bodvar. I know for sure someone got away last night, and he will have told men about your trip. I want nothing to happen to you since you have sought shelter from me."

Bodvar said, "I won't use it," and bid him farewell.

But soon they turned off the path and took the main road. Sigmund spotted them and went back to Bjorn and his men. He said, "I've seen them.

They're in front of us." They they quickly chased after them and caught up with them in the brushwood up from Hal's farm between the farms and Hella where Narfi lived.

"Men are coming," said Bodvar. "what do they want?"

Bersi answered, "They're up to no good. It looks live we must be drowned near land."

Bodvar said, "We must not run."

Bersi answered, "I don't mean to. We'll wait here."

There were seven in their band. Bodvar, Bersi and the ship's helmsman were in the lead. Bjorn's band had eleven altogether, but Thorstein said, "We must plan our attack. We can't see how it will turn out for sure. They're hard-bitten men and they have a natural stronghold. Some of us should attack at their back--but you stay here Thorgrim."

Just then a great man leaped towards Bodvar's men from the rear. It seemed that Eyjolf Thorsteinson had also come along! At this point Bodvar said, "We'll hold up here and defend ourselves."

Bjorn was first in the attack. Thorstein threw a spear at Havard, the Norwegian, and it landed in his belly. Bodvar yanked that spear out of Havard and sent it back, killing Thorstein. At this moment Eyjolf came up behind Bodvar and struck him his deathblow. After this, Eyjolf grabbed Bersi and ran sliding on the ice back into Bjorn's band, telling Bjorn to attack with him. Then he leaped at Bersi, cut him down, and said, "You have done well all by yourself, Eyjolf!" Bersi had slain Sigmund before.

In this battle, Bodvar, Bersi, Havard the Norwegian, and one other from their band fell dead. Thorstein and Sigmund from the Svarfadalers also died. Those left sent word to Narfi asking him to bring back the bodies. He felt bad about this for he was a friend to both sides. He rode to Modruvale and told Gudmund. Gudmund said this was a great misfortune. Meanwhile, Bjorn and Eyjolf made their plan. Eyjolf said it would be wise to go to Ljot.

He said, "Although bristling words may follow, there is still safety with Ljot. He'll help me, and I'm not going to stay here with you if you don't want to go, because you can't help me."

Bjorn said Ljot had warned that no blood revenge take place, but Eyjolf answered that the more need they had for backing, the more backing Ljot would give them, and he added, "The truth is, this blood revenge came mostly from our doing!"

Then they went to find Ljot and they told him they had avenged their kinsman.

Ljot said, "It isn't good to have rash kinsmen. They come here in bewilderment when the steps they've taken aren't good ones."

They all went to find Thorgrim, and Ljot asked, "Why did you host our enemies, Thorgrim, my kinsman?"

He answered, "It befitted me to do so. Though it hardly matters now, what I did rests with me, and what Sigmund did rests with him. But things have come a long way from what I had hoped."

Ljot said, "It would be better if it had gone as you hoped. Now I don't think it's wise for you to stay at your farm between Tjarn and Upsir. I think it's best that we all stay together, otherwise you'll be slain just like the white fox, in his lair. We must help you in this, and I shall take it on myself. While I don't want more killing to follow, still it's bad to lose face to any man."

Thorgrim said, "But what shall we do about Eyjolf, who is now most bound up in the case and the slayings?"

Ljot answered, "He can stay with me at first. Later, I'll send him south to Hjalla and from there he can go abroad. I'll send three of the others to Hermund Illugason and two to Thorkel Eyjolfson. If they aren't around, it might be easier to make a settlement. But Bjorn must stay with me. We will share the same fate."

Chapter 8--Gudmund and His Spear

All of this was done. Eyjolf left Iceland and became a Thingman of the English king. Narfi spoke to Gudmund about all this, and it seemed to Gudmund the more he learned the worse it got, yet he went out to the coast with Narfi, to a feast, to learn all about the matter.

Gudmund said, "They will be well-spoken of and their death is a great shame. They defended themselves so well, and they were guiltless. The Svarfadalers' esteem has risen now, and they should be content with this. How are Bjorn and Thorgrim guarding themselves now?"

Narfi answered, "Bjorn stays at home with a few men, and so does Thorgrim."

Gudmund said, "Thorgrim did well in this business, but is their chieftain, Ljot, also on guard?"

He said that Ljot would be on guard.

"I'm not happy," said Gudmund, "with the way things stand. I want your help to search through the valley and see if we can catch some of them."

Narfi said he would help, adding, "I'm ready right now, and all the secret paths are known to me. Still, such a plan must have luck to succeed."

Gudmund said he would risk it anyway, and they went out into the valley.

Narfi said, "Ljot often rides with his men on the upper road and comes down from it at his farm."

Gudmund said, "We'll stay here and wait, but you go to the farm and see what you can find out."

Ljot's sheep pen was a short way from them. Narfi came back with the news that all Ljot's kinsmen were at the farm for a feast--they hadn't known that before!

It was Ljot's usual habit to get up early to see to his work and cattle. Gudmund and his men waited in the woods on a tongue of land between two glens. They saw a man leave the farmhouse wearing a dark cape and holding a battle-ax in his hand. He went to the sheep pen and drove out the sheep. Then Gudmund told his men to run up and grab him, but not to use weapons on him.

Ljot saw them, turned around, and ran towards the glen with the battle-ax in his hand. He leaped into the glen, and since there was ice underfoot, he slid all the way down. He wasn't hurt.

Gudmund said, "There he goes!" and threw a spear after him, but it only hit his battle-ax. Ljot picked up the spear and went home. Gudmund went back to the woods and said, "Ljot is skillful, and such men fare well. He's not a troublemaker, but a brave man and shrewd. He took the only way out and he must have known before that he could escape that way. We'll wait now and see what he means to do. We'll not turn away even though staying here is rash indeed."

When Ljot came home he kept the spear--it was inlaid with gold. Later his men asked where it had come from. Ljot answered, "Gudmund the Mighty sent it to me." They asked who brought it, and Ljot said Gudmund trusted no one in this matter, adding, "He sent it himself." They said he had hidden this too long. He said that wasn't so.

"I knew," said Ljot, "that I couldn't have got you to calm down if you had known of this before, and it would have been hard to fight the Eyjafirthers, too great a task."

Ljot didn't start a case for this attack on his life.

The time for the Althing came, and many men were there, including the North-Quartermen, Ljot and Gudmund. Gudmund came with a manslaughter suit against Ljot. The men went to seek out a settlement. The friends of Ljot and Gudmund met and talked about it. Ljot told them all his dealings with Gudmund. He added, "We'll go talk to him. If we can put things right then I won't take up a case for his attack on me."

Skapti answered, "You have done rightly in this, and I'll support you in everything."

"To be sure," said Ljot, "but when I fled from them, I thought I shouldn't wait around to find out what others were saying about this matter! Now I also want you to bring the spear to Gudmund."

Skapti agreed and asked Ljot to go with him to Gudmund. Ljot said he would.

Gudmund greeted Skapti and said, "Why are you helping Ljot and his followers?"

Skapti saud, "It has turned out that way, but I do it not for hatred of you, but only because Ljot wanted you to have this spear. He said you sent it."

Gudmund answered, "I little intended to honor you, Ljot, when I sent you that spear."

"It has since come about," said Ljot, "that I do not mean to profit by this spear."[20]

Gudmund said he was all for that, and he added, "You must take this sword." -- it was a very costly sword.

Then Ljot said to Gudmund, "Accept this sword from me, but don't send me another spear in the same way and we can thus end our case. That way you still hold your honor, and we can end our quarrel."

"It shall be so," said Gudmund.

Bjorn wasn't at the Thing because he had been sent out to Grim's Island at Ljot's behest. He was hidden there by a man named Thrand. Bjorn told him Ljot's message that he had been sent out there for safety and help while the Thing was going on. Bjorn added, "Ljot will end the suit for me."

Thrand said he would help as best he could.

Chapter 9--Hrolf Breaks the Settlement

Hrolf was at home when the case was settled at the Thing. At the Thing, Ljot said he wanted to offer exile and heavy fines. Many of the lesser men were against this settlement, but the rest thought it was good that Ljot settled in a way that honored Gudmund. It happened that Ljot wanted Skapti to set judgment on his behalf, but Gudmund wanted to set the judgment himself. It was done that way, and they were both pleased with it. Skapti told the judgment aloud, and there were many men to hear it.

Skapti said, "In this matter we'll count as equal the ambush of Bodvar and Sigmund's death, Bersi's slaying and Thorstein's. For the slaying of the trader, two hundred ounces of silver, and for the death of Bodvar, the same sum must be paid as was paid before for the slaying of Thorvard. Nine men will not be allowed to return to Iceland. Bjorn must pay a hundred for his freedom and he must spend two years away."

They all agreed to this.

Meanwhile, Bjorn was quite safe on the island with Thrand. One day during the Thing, Bjorn was eager to row out with Thrand and fish, but Thrand said there was no need to do this, adding, I don't want the man Ljot sent to me to be ambushed, and there is less safety to be found on boats than on an island."

"It won't hurt to do it," said Bjorn, and that day with thirty boats, all small, they rowed out from the island. The weather was good, and the men were cheerful because the ships lay near each other.

Then Thrand said, "There's a ship going in along the fjord, and I think it's Gudmund's ferry. Who might be on it? Do you know whether Hrolf the Greedy is at the Thing?"

The fishermen answered that he might be at home.

Then Thrand said, "He'll come here to find you, Bjorn, and you'll be found because the men here won't be silent, and we'll defend ourselves poorly with only small boats. They have a great ship and many men. At any rate we must make ready for them even though we have only a little chance."

They started rowing back towards the island.

The men on Hrolf's ship saw this and said, "They're rowing fast, away from the fishing bank now. They must suspect us."

Hrolf answered, "Go after them!" They did so and quickly caught up with them. Hrolf asked whether Bjorn was in one of the small boats.

Thrand answered, "What do you think?"

Hrolf said, "Give him up. Don't risk your lives and your goods. You haven't the men for that, and don't make trouble and cause a suit to be brought against you."

Thrand answered, "You're not playing a good part in this matter when you set yourself up over a chieftain, and trouble will come from this. You aren't backing your chieftain, and when you break such a settlement you are going to kindle up again the chieftains' full anger. I know also that you have fixed for Bjorn the same fate as his brother, and you're to blame for all these slayings. Haven't you heard from the Thing? Aren't men now at peace? Is this your custom--to settle first, then slay men later? You'll not take him easily!"

"We'll take him, all right," said Hrolf, "and slay you!"

Thrand answered, "Will you take money?"

Hrolf answered, "I must set the amount."

Then Bjorn said, "Self-judgment is no good. Let's risk a fight."

Thrand told him, "We aren't short of money, but we can hardly get another man as good as you."

Bjorn said much was still to happen before they caught him. Thrand said he wanted to end this matter, and he added, "It's now my business."

Hrolf said, "You must pay up right now two hundred ounces of silver for Bjorn."

Thrand answered, "The payment will cause us hardship," but the fishermen paid off the money to him and went home penniless. So parted Thrand and Hrolf.

Ljot came home from the Thing and met Bjorn. They talked about what had happened. Ljot said Thrand wasn't to be blamed. He also said, "Hrolf has shown his usual greedy self, but now he must be at ease. We must pay Gudmund two hundred silvers at the meeting. We will pay this but not the other two hundred since Hrolf and his men will have to hand them over to Gudmund in disgrace."

Ljot sent a message to Gudmund and told him Hrolf's act was a clear challenge, and he asked him to control Hrolf. Gudmund said it would be done. He said Hrolf had often steered him towards dishonor.

Gudmund paid back all the money to the island men. Ljot settled matters himself between Thrand and Gudmund, and they were well-pleased and thought Ljot to be the greatest chieftain. So ended Ljot's dealings with Gudmund the Mighty. Gudmund was honored until he died, and so ends this saga.

Notes on the Saga of Valla Ljot

[1]Thorfi is Eyjolf's Thingman. Gudmund, Eyjolf's son, is Gudmund the Mighty, a principal character in the saga.

[2]Freedom could be given slaves or it could be bought for them. Slavery as an institutional aspect of Icelandic society disappeared around 1100.

[3]The term used here means "winter-nights." It refers to the three days which begin the winter season, starting with the Saturday of the week of October 11-17.

[4]What Halli here calls a "taunting" insult was a legal phrase denoting an insult punishable under the law.

[5]A "hundred," here and throughout these sagas refers to the Germanic or "great hundred" of 120.

[6]Primesigning was a custom of making the sign of the cross over the forehead. It was usually a preliminary to baptism.

[7]A metaphorical term, suggesting that Halli zealously supported Gudmund's legal actions.

[8]Allusions to specific events which are not subsequently explained are fairly common in the sagas and are often cited as evidence for an oral tradition behind the sagas.

[9]Asking permission to settle was a courtesy. Halli, by virtue of his social standing, would not be refused if he asked, and by not asking he is behaving discourteously.

[10]Not the aforementioned Hrolf Sigurdson.

[11]The 29th of September.

[12]Michael.

[13]The formal duel was prohibited shortly after the official adoption of Christianity, possibly because the practice involved sacrifices and other pagan rites. Presumably, Bersi now finds it more

comfortable to leave since under the law he cannot challenge Ljot to single combat to avenge his father.

[14]This fjord borders both Svarfadale and Modruvale.

[15]He means Gudmund's men.

[16]To claim payment in Olafsfjord, they would have to travel through Svarfadale. That, of course, would be Gudmund's greatest concern.

[17]The brother of Valla Ljot.

[18]Bjorn Thorgrimson, nephew of Valla Ljot.

[19]Thus right past Svarfadale.

[20]Probably by using it as evidence cf Gudmund's attack on him.

THE STORY OF THORVARD CROW NOSE

Thorvard Crow Nose was a West Fjord man by birth. He was a wealthy man and also noble-minded. He had journeyed through many lands, and was highly thought of wherever he went. One summer he took his ship north to Nidaros. At that time King Harald was staying there, and with him was Eystein Orri, his brother-in-law, the son of Thorberg Arnason.[1] Of all men Eystein was the bravest and the most honored by the King.

Thorvard unloaded his boat and rented himself a room. Then he went to the drinking hall to find King Harald. When he came to the hall, the King was outside, but when he started to go back in, Thórvard said, "Hail, lord! Here is a sail from my ship which I wish you would accept."

The king frowned somewhat and said, "Once I accepted a sail from you Icelanders and it almost did me in. It ripped apart at sea. I won't take it."

Eystein said, "Go over and look at it, lord. It might please you. The odds are good such a man would give you a worthy gift."

The King said, "You know what's best for you, but I know what's best for me."

Then he went into the hall and said no more about it.

Thorvard then said to Eystein, "Come here," and he asked him to accept the sail. Eystein went over and he thought he had never seen a greater treasure in a sail. He thanked Thorvard well for the gift and asked him to visit his farm on the island of Gizki, in the North district, during the winter.

Nothing much happened during the winter, but when spring came, Thorvard got his ship ready nd sailed south along the coast. Near Solskel he had to wait for a good wind, and one day he saw a ship sailing up to him quickly, under a full sail. It was fully manned from stem to stern. A handsome and stately man stood up in the prow. He wore a scarlet tunic. He asked if Thorvard were aboard. Thorvard answered and gave Eystein a good welcome.

Eystein said, "You are slow in seeking my home. Come aboard with us with as many of your men as you wish, because the wind is not promising now."

Thorvard did so, and went over with a few men. His ship was rowed to the island of Gizki, and there a great welcome feast was held. Eystein's home was a good one, and very large. When the afternoon and night had passed and morning had come, Thorvard awoke to see Eystein standing at his feet.

Eystein said, "The wind is not fair. Stay with us today, and let me look out for the wind for you. It's bound to turn soon."

Later on in the day, after they had drunk and were merry, Eystein said to Thorvard, "For coming with me willingly from your ship and seeking out my home, accept from me this tunic." Thorvard thanked him for the gift.

Eystein said, "This is not a reward for the sail."

Thorvard stayed for the day, and no one lacked good drink.

The next morning, Eystein said to Thorvard, "You shall rest again today, for there is no wind."

Thorvard said, "Then you must look out for it." Whereupon there was even greater feasting and drinking, and at one point Eystein took off his coat. It was pure gray fur, carefully sewn, and had a scarlet cloak fastened to it.

Eystein said, "You must accept this coat as reward for the sail, for it surpasses most other coats as the sail surpasses most other sails."

Thorvard thanked him well for the gift. The night passed, and early in the morning Thorvard was awakened by Eystein. He said, "I shall not hold you back today, for a fair wind has come."

They ate and drank before they left, and Eystein said to Thorvard, "It was not fated to happen that the King would accept your sail, but I guess, that if he had taken it, he would have rewarded you as I have done. Still, you're not yet rewarded enough for it, because it wasn't the king who repaid you, but me, and though it's not my fault that I'm not as high-born as the King, for our difference in rank you must take this gold ring"--and he drew it from his hand.

Thorvard thanked him for the ring and after that went down to his ship. The wind was fair, and he sailed out to Iceland, where he became a great man.

In the summer, when King Harald and Eystein sailed together along the coast of Norway, Eystein sailed faster and overtook the King.

The King said, "From where did you get such a good sail?"

Eystein answered, "This is the sail you refused, lord."

The King said, "I have never seen a better sail, and I have surely refused a good thing."

Eystein said, "Would the sail be worth a kiss, lord?"

The King smiled. "Why not?" he said, and went over to the mast.

Eystein said, "Don't humble yourself. Take the sail whenever you want it. It is well you should be reminded of what a treasure you once refused."

The King thanked him and mounted the sail on his ship. But it could never help the King's ship in a sailing match, because the King's ship was too large for it--though it had seemed to be the greatest treasure.

Note on The Story of Thorvard Crow Nose

+Harald Sigurdson (Hard-Ruler) married Thora, daughter of Thorberg Arnason, sister of Eystein Orri. Eystein Orri was later to lead a famous last charge for Harald at the Battle of Stamford Bridge.

THE STORY OF SHUTTLE HALLI

Chapter 1---King Harald and Thjodolf

This saga begins when King Harald Sigurdson ruled Norway. That was after the death of his kinsman, King Magnus.[1] It is said that of all men King Harald was the wisest and shrewdest. Whatever he did usually turned out well. He was also a good skald. He was always throwing taunts at men whenever he felt like it, yet he suffered it as the best of men when taunts were thrown at him--when he was in a good mood. He married Thora, duaghter of Thorberg Arnason. For Harald, skaldship was a great enjoyment, and he always kept those with him, who knew how to make poems.

There was once an Icelander named Thjodolf, from Svarfadardale by birth. He was a noble man and a great skald, and he was the greatest of friends with King Harald. The King valued him most of all the skalds and made him the chief skald. Thjodolf was not of high birth, yet he was skilled in many things, and resented the other skalds with King Harald.[2]

King Harald greatly loved Icelanders. He gave Iceland many good things, such as a good bell for Thingvellir, and when a famine came to Iceland so great there hasn't been one like it since, he sent to Iceland four cargo ships laden with flour, one to each quarter, and he had brought back to Norway as many of the poor as possible.

Chapter 2--Halli Answers the King

One of King Harald's men was a man called Bard. He sailed to Iceland and landed at Gasar, where he spent the winter. There a man named Halli took return passage with him. This man was called Shuttle Halli. He was a good skald, quite skilled with words. Halli was a tall man with a long neck, narrow shoulders, and long and misshapen arms. He was from Fljot by birth.

They sailed as soon as they were ready and had a long voyage. They reached Norway in the autumn north of Trondheim at the Hit islands. From there they sailed to Agdaness where they anchored for the night. In the morning they sailed into the fjord with a little breeze, and when they got near Rein, they saw three longships rowing out to meet them.

The third ship was a warship, and when this ship came alongside theirs, a man came forward from the quarter-deck, wearing scarlet clothes and a gold lace headband. He was a large and lordly man, and he said, "Who's the master of this ship? Where did you spend the winter? Where did you first make land? Where did you anchor last night.?"

The men in the trading ship were nearly struck dumb by so many questions at once, but Halli answered, "We were in Iceland for the winter; put to sea from Gasar; Bard is our ship's master; landed at Hit; and spent the night at Agdaness."

The man, who was really King Harald Sigurdson, asked, "Did Agdi not mount you?"[4]

"Not yet," said Halli.

The King smiled and said, "Isn't it likely that he will pay you this favor later on?"

"No," said Halli, "there is a very good reason why we won't get such shame from him."

"What's that?" said the King. Halli knew for sure to whom he was speaking.

"That, lord," he said, "if you really want to

know, is this--Agdi waits for nobler men than us, and he expects you in the evening. Then he will pay the favor in full."

"You're a brash man," said the King. There was no more said at that time.

The traders sailed to Nidaros, unloaded there, and rented themselves a house in town. A few nights later the King returned. He had been in the outer islands to amuse himself. Halli asked Bard to bring him to the King. He wanted to ask for winter-quarters. Bard asked Halli to stay with him, and Halli thanked him for this, but said he wanted to stay with the King if it were possible.

Chapter 3--Halli Joins the King's Men

One day Bard went to the King and took Halli with him. Bard greeted the King and was welcomed by him. The King asked much about Iceland, and whether Bard had brought any Icelanders with him. Bard said he had brought out one Icelander and he added, "His name is Halli, and he is here now, lord, to ask you for winter-quarters."

Halli then went before the King and greeted him. The King welcomed him and asked whether he had answered him in the fjord--"When we last met," he said.

"You're looking at the same man," said Halli.

The King said he wouldn't deny him food, and asked Halli to stay with him a while. Halli said he wanted to join the King's men or he would look elsewhere.

The King said, "Always am I blamed if a friendship doesn't turn out well, and that seems hardly right to me. You Icelanders are selfwilled and unfriendly. Now, if you want to stay here, we shall hold you solely answerable for your deeds, whatever happens."

Halli said so it should be, and thanked the King.

Halli then joined the King's men, and everyone liked him very much. His benchmate's name was Sigurd, an older man and quiet. It was then the custom of King Harald to eat one meal a day. The food was first set before the King, as was customary, and by the time it was set before the others, the King was already greatly filled. When he had had enough, the King clapped his knife handle on the table, and at once the tables were cleared, but many men were nowhere near finished.

One time, before many of his men had even begun to finish eating, the King had his men go out into the street with him. In one building they heard a great quarrel. It was a tanner and an ironsmith and they had nearly come to blows. The King waited a while, and then he said, "We must leave. I want no part of this. But you, Thjodolf, compose a poem about them."

"Lord," said Thjodolf, "I am your head skald, and this doesn't befit me."

The King said, "This will be harder than you think. You must make both of them other than what they are. Let one be Sigurd Fafnisbana, and the other Fafnir, but show them each in their own craft."

Thjodolf then spoke this poem:

Iron-Hammer Sigurd goaded
The awful Scraper-Serpent,
While the Skin-Scraper Dragon
Slithered over the Foot-Heath (tanning pit)
Men feared the Dragon,
Before the Shoe-Leather-Snake
By the long-nosed
King of tongs was slain.

"That was well-done," said the King, "now make another one. This time let one be Thor and the other the giant,[5] Geirrod, but show each of them in their own craft.

Thjodolf spoke this verse:

Threw from his quarrel-home (mouth)
Thor a great bellows blast,
Mouth-flames, to the
Goat-skin giant.
Hide-Scraper Geirrod
Gladly with sound-grippers (ears)
Took the glowing iron
From his word-smith. (mouth)

"It's not said in vain that you are a master of skaldship," said the King. Everyone praised it and said it was well-made. Halli wasn't there for this, but in the evening, when men sat drinking, they called for Halli and told him he couldn't do as well even though he thought himself a great skald.

Halli said he knew he would do worse than Thjodolf, but he added, "I would suffer more if I were there and didn't try." This was at once told to the King, but twisted so that it came out as though Halli thought himself no less a skald than Thjodolf. The King thought that wasn't likely, but he added, "Yet I know we'll get a trial of this before long."

Chapter 4--Halli and his Porridge

One day while the men were at the table, there came into the hall a dwarf called Tuta. He was a Frisian by birth, but had long been with King Harald. He was no taller than a three year old child, but of all men he was the stoutest and broadest of shoulder. His head was large and wrinkled. His back was fairly long, but his legs were very short and stocky.

Now King Harald had a coat of mail which he called Emma. It had been made for him in Miklagard,[6] and it was so long that it came down to his shoes when he stood upright. It was all doubled and so strong that iron never pierced it. The King made the dwarf wear the coat of mail, and he put a helmet on his head and girded on him a sword. This dwarf went into the hall, as was said before, and this sight seemed to the men a wondrous thing.

The King then called for silence and said, "That man who makes a verse about a dwarf that seems to me well-made shall get from me this knife and belt," and he laid across the table in front of him the costly treasures. "But know for sure," he added, "that if the verse seems to me not well-made, then he shall have my anger and shall miss both treasures."

As soon as the King had stated this, a man way out on the bench recited a verse, and that man was Shuttle Halli.

I think I see the Frisian
All clad in mail.
Under helm, the coal-cutter*
Walks before the King's men.
Used to food raids, Tuta
Flees not the morning fire.
A sword, I see, hangs at
The rye loaf carver's side.

*Fire maker, a menial task.

The King bade the treasures be brought to Halli, and he added, "You truly deserve these, for the verse was well-made."

One day when the King had finished eating, he clapped his knife on the table and ordered it cleared. The serving men did so, but Halli was nowhere near finished, He then took a chop from his dish, held it up and said this:

I'll pay no heed,
When Harald claps;
Let the pine board ring
When I go full to bed.

The morning after, when the King and his men had taken their seats, Halli entered the hall and went up to the King. He had his shield and sword on his back. He spoke this verse:

For butter, my sword
Must I sell, O King,
And my red shield
For bread, O shield-roar maker (warrior)
Warriors hunger, O King.

Quite slender we become.
Belts nearly pinch backbones.
Harald starves me!

The King didn't answer. He pretended he didn't hear, but it was clear to everyone that he wasn't pleased. One day a little later, the King and his men left the hall and went out into the street. Halli started out with them, but he quickly ran away from the King.

The King said, "Why are you sneaking away, Halli?"

Halli answered, "I'm running away to buy curds."

The King said, "Are you going to make porridge?"

Halli answered, "With butter, that's a good meal!"

Halli then ran into a yard where there was a cook-house. There he made porridge in a stone kettle and sat down and ate it. The King had seen where Halli turned into the yard. He told Thjodolf and two other men to look for Halli there, and the King also went towards the yard. Thjodolf and the men found him right where he was eating porridge. Then the King came up and also saw what he was doing. The King got very angry and asked Halli why he had left Iceland to become one of the King's men if all he was doing was making a shame and mockery of himself.

"Don't talk that way, lord," said Halli, "I never see you refuse a good meal." Halli then stood up and threw down the kettle so that the handle clanged loudly. Whereupon Thjodolf said this:

The handle rings loud,
But Halli's glutted on porridge.
He listens better, I think,
To the hornspoon, than his pride.

The King went away very angry, and in the evening no meat was set before Halli as before the others. After the men had eaten a while, two men came in, carrying between themselves a great trough, full of porridge, with a spoon in it. They set it before Halli. Halli started eating. He ate what he wanted, and then he stopped. The King told Halli to eat more. Halli said he wouldn't eat any more just now. Whereupon King Harald drew his sword and ordered Halli to eat the porridge until he burst from it. Halli said he wouldn't burst himself with porridge, but he said the King could have his life if he were so minded. The King sheathed his sword.

Chapter 5--Halli Thinks Quickly

One day a little later on the King took a dish from his table with a roasted pig on it and told Tuta, the dwarf, to take it to Halli, and he added, "Tell him to make a verse, if he wishes to live, and to have made it before you get to him, and tell him this not before you get to the middle of the floor."

"I'm not eager for this," said Tuta, "because I like Halli well."

"I guess," said the King, "you think he made a good verse about you. You really have a skillful ear! Now go away at once, and do what I told you."

Tuta took the dish, went to the middle of the floor and said, "Halli, by the King's command you must make a verse, and you must make it before I get to you, if you want to hold your life."

Halli stood up, reached for the dish, and spoke this verse:

The skald accepts the dead pig
From the noble chieftain.
Njord's shield sees the boar (Halli)
On the table before him stand.
The red ham steaks I see;
Only make a quick poem,
Seared nose boar to have.
All thanks to the King!

Whereupon the King said, "Now I must lose my anger at you, Halli, for the verse was well-made, and all the more since it was done so quickly."

Chapter 6--Halli Spars with Thjodolf

It is said that one day Halli went before the King when the King was cheerful and merry. Thjodolf and many others were there. Halli said he had made a *drápa* about the King and asked him to listen. The King asked whether Halli had made such poems before. Halli said he hadn't.

"Then some men would say," said the King, "that you take too much in hand, for skalds have made such poems about me many times before. But what do you think, Thjodolf?"

"I can not give you advice, lord," said Thjodolf, "but it's very clear that I can give Halli some good counsel."

"What is that?" said the King.

"That above all, he should not lie to you," said Thjodolf.

"How did he lie?" said the King.

"He lied when he said he had not made such poems before," said Thjodolf, "but I say he has."

"What poems were they," said the King, and on what were they made?"

Thjodolf answered, "We call them Cow poems. He made them about cattle he watched over in Iceland."

"Is that true, Halli," said the King.

"It is true," said Halli.

"Why did you say you hadn't made such poems before?" said the King.

"Because," said Halli, "if men knew that, the poem would be little valued and little praised."

"We must first hear it," said the King.

"But this you will enjoy more," said Halli.

"What's that?" said the King.

"Thjodolf should recite a Swill Trough poem, which he used to make in Iceland," said Halli, "and it is well that Thjodolf should try to mock and shame me, for now my teeth are bared, and I shall answer him with equal words."

The King smiled and thought it sport to urge them on. "What kind of poem will it be. and about what will it tell?" said the King.

Halli answered, "It will be about those days when he carried the ashes out of his house with his sisters, for no one thought him clever enough for anything else. He had to watch out for live coals, and for that he needed all his wit."

The King asked if this were true.

"It is true, lord," said Thjodolf.

"Why did you have such unworthy work?" said the King.

"Because, lord," said Thjodolf, "I wanted only to get to the games sooner. The work wasn't given to me as my job."

"The reason for that was," said Halli, "that you didn't have the wit for it."

"You shall quarrel no more," said the King, "we must hear both of you compose."

So it was. Each recited his poem, and when the poems were done, the King said, "Neither poem is very good, and they speak of unworthy things, but yours is the worst, Thjodolf."

"So it is," said Thjodolf, "and Halli is very sharp-tongued, but it seems to me he would be better off avenging his father than bandying words with me here in Norway."

"Is that true, Halli?" said the King.

"It's true, lord," said Halli.

"Why did you leave Iceland to join us if you

hadn't avenged your father?" said the King.

"Because, lord," said Halli, "I was only a child when my father was slain. My kinsman took up the case and settled it for me, and it is bad to have the name of peace-breaker in a land."

The King answered, "There is a need not to break settlements, and you are well-cleared of this charge."

"So I thought, lord," said Halli, "but well can Thjodolf speak with great pride about such things, for I know of no one who so fiercely avenged his father as he."

"For sure, Thjodolf is likely to have done that bravely," said the King, "but what did he do that was more than others would have done?"

"This most of all, lord," said Halli, "he ate his father's slayer!"

At this, the men broke out in laughter. They thought they had never heard such a strange thing. The King smiled and told the men to be quiet.

"Prove what you said, Halli," said the King.

Halli said, "I think Thjodolf's father was named Thorljot. He lived in Svarfadardale in Iceland, and he had many children and was very poor. It was then the custom in Iceland to have a Thing called for the poor men, and there were none poorer than Thorljot, Thjodolf's father. At the Thing one householder was so generous he gave Thorljot a year old calf. Later, he led the calf away by a rope. There was a loop in the end of the rope which he held. When he got to his home meadow turf wall, he lifted the calf up on top of the wall. The wall was very high, but it was higher still on the inside, because on that side had been dug all the turf for the wall. Thorljot went over the wall to the inside. Just then the calf fell off the wall to the outside, and the loop on the rope caught Thorljot round the neck and pulled his feet off the ground. Now each one hung on his side of the wall, and they both died before they were found. The children dragged the calf home and made a meal out of it, and I'm sure Thjodolf got his fair share."

"Quite likely," said the King.

Thjodolf drew his sword and wanted to cut Halli down, but men leaped between them. The King said it wouldn't do for either of them to harm the other, and he added, "You, Thjodolf, offended Halli first."

It came to be as the King wished. Halli recited the *drápa* and did it well, and the King rewarded him with a lot of money. Thus the winter passed and all was quiet.

Chapter 7--Halli and Einar the Fly

There was a man named Einar who was called "The Fly". He was the son of Harek from Thjotta. He was a landed man and held the King's stewardship in Halogaland. He also traded with the Finns. He was very good friends with the King, though there were ups and downs in their friendship. Einar was a very brutal man. He slew men if they didn't do everything he wanted, and he paid atonement for no one. Men knew that he would stay with the King's men at Yule. Halli and Sigurd, his benchmate, talked about Einar. Sigurd said to Halli that no one dared speak against Einar, or cross him in any way, and that he paid no compensation for his killings and robbery.

Halli answered, "He would be called an awful scoundrel in our land."

"Speak carefully, good friend," said Sigurd, "because he is easily offended by words that don't suit his mood."

"Even though he looms so large that none of you dare say one word to cross him, I'll tell you this," said Halli, "I'll charge him if he does me wrong, and I'll bet that he will compensate me."

"Why you, and not the others?" said Sigurd.

"He will think it better to do so," said Halli.

They argued about this until Halli asked Sigurd to bet on it. Sigurd put up a gold ring which weighed half a mark, but Halli put up his head.

Einar came at Yule, and he sat opposite the King, with his men on either side. He was served as was the King himself. Yule day, when the men had eaten their fill, the King said, "Now we will have more sport than just drinking. Einar, you must tell us about your journey."

Einar answered, "I can't make that into a good story, lord, for we only beat up some Finnish farmers and fishermen."

The King answered, "Tell it in more detail. Though it seems to you of little worth, since you're always in trouble, there may be sport in it."

"The best part," said Einar, "was last summer when we went north to Finnmark. There we met an Icelandic ship. They had been blown off course and stayed there for the winter. I charged them with trading with the Finns without your leave, or mine. They denied this, and said it wasn't so. But I thought they were lying, and demanded a search. This they flatly refused. Whereupon I told them they deserved the worst, and told my men to arm themselves and attack. I had five longships. We attacked and didn't let up before their ship was cleared. But one Icelander, whom they called Einar, defended himself so well that his match I have never found. Surely the death of this man was a great pity, and we would never have taken the ship if all aboard had been like him."

"You don't do well, Einar, to slay guiltless men just because they won't do as you ask," said the King.

"I shall not," said Einar, "shoulder their peril--and some men say, lord, that you aren't the most just in everything. Besides, they proved to be guilty, for we found many Finnish wares in the ship."

Halli heard what they said. He threw his knife from the table and stopped eating. Sigurd asked if he were sick. Halli said he wasn't sick, that this was worse than sickness.

"Einar the Fly," he said, "has told of the the death of Einar, my brother--when he said he ambushed a trading ship last summer. Perhaps there is now a chance to get compensation from this Einar."

"Say nothing about it, good friend," said Sigurd, "that is the best way."

"No," said Halli, "my brother would hardly do such a thing if I were slain." Whereupon he jumped up from the table, went before the high seat, and said, "Your tale, peasant Einar, when you said you had fallen on a trading ship last summer, concerns me greatly -- in the slaying of Einar, my brother! I want to know, now, whether you will make atonement for my brother, Einar."

"Have you not heard," said Einar, "that I pay compensation for no man?"

"There is no need for me to believe," said Halli, "that you would be given to such evil, though I have heard that said."

"Go away man," said Einar, "or it will be the worse for you."

Halli went to his seat. Sigurd asked how he had fared. Halli answered and he said that he had gotten only threats for compensation. Sigurd asked him not to take up the case again and asaid he would release him from their wager. Halli said that was good of him, but he added, "I must do it again."

Another day Halli went before Einar and said, "I want to raise the case of whether you will make atonement for my brother."

Einar answered, "You are thick-headed, and if you don't go away, you shall make the same trip your brother did -- or worse."

The King told him not to answer in that way, and he added, "That is too great a trial of kinship, and no one knows how he will take it. But you, Halli, do not bring up this case again, for it will take a mightier man than you are to carry this to Einar."

Halli answered, "So it must be," and he went back to his seat. Sigurd welcomed himand asked how he had fared. Halli said he got threats as atonement from Einar.

"I thought so," said Sigurd, "and I release you from the wager."

"That's good of you," said Halli, "but I must go a third time."

"I will give you the ring now," said Sigurd, "so you will no longer stir this up. All this started with me."

Halli answered, "You show what kind of man you are, but this is not on your shoulders, however it goes -- and I must try still once more."

The next morning, while the King and Einar washed their hands, Halli went and greeted the King. The King asked what he wanted.

"Lord," said Halli, I want to tell you about my dream. I seemed to be wholly someone else."

"What man did you seem to be?" said the King.

"I seemed to be skald Thorleif and Einar the Fly seemed to me to be Jarl Hakon Sigurdson, and I seemed to have made a slanderous verse about him, and I remembered some of the verse when I woke up."[9] Whereupon Halli turned toward the entrance of the hall and muttered something that no one understood.

The King said, "That was not a real dream but a clever ruse that makes the two of you equal to Jarl Hakon of Lade and skald Thorleif, with Halli as Thorleif. He shrinks from nothing! And we see that the insult poem has bitten Jarl Hakon, a mightier man than you, Einar, and that will be remembered while Norway is settled. It is also worse if it lingers on in memory because little compensation is paid,so do the best thing now and send him off with something."

"Your will must be done, lord," said Einar, "tell him to take from my treasurer the three marks of silver in the little purse I gave him."

Halli was told of this. He went to the treasurer and made his demand. The treasurer said there were four marks of silver in the purse. Halli said he must have three. He then went back to Einar,who asked him, "Do you have what was in the purse?"

"No," said Halli, "you may get my life in other ways, but not as a thief of your money. I know that's what you planned for me." And so it was that Einar had meant for Halli to take what was in the purse, a deed Einar thought worthy of death.

Halli went back to his seat and showed Sigurd the money. Sigurd took off the ring and said Halli had won it bravely, but Halli said, "Then we won't have come out of this evenly. Take back your ring and use it as the best of men. To tell you the truth, I was never any kinsman of the man Einar slew. I just wanted to see if I could get money from him."

"No man is a better trickster than you," said Sigurd.

After Yule, Einar went north to Halogaland.

Chapter 8--Halli Goes to Denmark

In the spring Halli asked the King's leave to go to Denmark in a trading ship. The King told him to do as he wished, and he added, "But come back quickly, for we enjoy your company, and be careful of Einar the Fly. He will be out to get you, for seldom have I known him to have been taken so badly."

Halli took passage with some traders south towards Denmark. They landed in Jutland. There was a man named Raud who ran a district there, and Halli stayed with him. One day Raud held a well-attended Thing, but when men tried to speak their cases, there was such great noise and shouting, that no one could do it, and the men went home in the evening with nothing done. That night, as the men were drinking, Raud said, "He would be a shrewd man who found a way to get all these people to be quiet."

Halli answered, "I can make, in an instant, every person here shut up."

"That you will not succeed in doing, countryman," said Raud.

In the morning everyone came to the Thing, and there was the same uproar and shouting as before. The men went home with no cases decided. Afterwards, Raud said, "Will you wager, Halli, on whether you can get silence at the Thing?"

"So be it," said Halli.

In the morning Raud asked Halli if he wanted to try the bet that day. Halli said he did. Men came again to the Thing and there was soon as much noise or more than the day before. When it was at its worst, Halli leaped up and shouted as loud as he could, "Everyone listen! I have urgent words. I have lost a whetstone and whetstone grease, and a bag with everything in it -- all of which it's better for a man to have than to lose."

Everyone fell silent. Some thought he had gone mad, and some thought he spoke some message of the King's. While there was silence, Halli sat down and picked up the ring. But once men saw this was nothing but a joke, the shouting began again.

Halli ran away, for Raud wanted to kill him. He thought this had been the worst of tricks. Halli didn't stop until he got to England.

Chapter 9--Halli Goes to England

At this time Harold Godwinson ruled England.[10] Halli went at once to meet the King. He said he had made a <u>drápa</u> about him, and asked him to listen to it. The King granted him a hearing. Halli sat before the King's knee and recited the poem. When it was done, the King asked his skald, who was with him, how the poem was. He said he thought it was good. The King asked Halli to stay with him, but Halli said he had already made plans to go to Norway. The King said then that thus the poem should not be rewarded, and he added, "You should get as much by it as we do, and there's no honor in a poem none of us know by heart. So, sit down on the floor, and I will have silver poured on your head. You can keep what sticks in your hair. It seems to me this is a fair reward if the poem will not stay with us."

Halli answered, "It seems my poem is worth little if this is the reward. But would you let me, lord, go out and relieve myself?"

"Go if you wish," said the King.

Halli went right to where some shipbuilders were. He put tar on his head and shaped his hair into a dish, then he went back and asked them to pour silver over him. The King said he was cunning, but the silver was poured over him, and he kept quite a bit of it.

Halli went then to where the Norway-bound ships were. They were all away but one, and that one already had many men and much cargo. But Halli had the money and he really wanted to leave, because in fact he had only composed a nonsense poem about the King, and he worried that the King would find out. The ship's master said he would be glad to take him if he could find some way to get the southern men to leave the ship.[11]

By this time the weather had worsened, and Halli stayed with these men in a lodging for a time. One night Halli was very restless in his sleep, and it was long before the men could wake him. They asked what he had dreamed. Halli said the result of it was that he was going to pray for them on the voyage.

He said, "It seemed that a fearsome man came to me and said this:

Storms rage where, in death,
I grasp the tall seaweed.
Beside Ran I dwell; (a sea-goddess)
Some with lobsters stay.
The nights I spend with fish,

My homestead is far from shore.
Pale I am as the seaweed,
It twists about my neck.
It twists about my neck.

When the southern men thought about this dream, they decided to leave the ship. They thought it meant death to sail on it. Halli then went aboard at once, and said that it had only been a trick of his, and no dream. They sailed when ready, and made Norway in the autumn. Halli went at once to King Harald. The King greeted Halli well and asked if he made any poems about other kings. Halli said this:

A nonsense verse
For a Jarl I made.
Drápas are done
No worse among the Danes.[12]
Fourteen rifts were there,
And ten riders.
Open at the start,
At the end, rising.
All done as though
One didn't know how.

The King smiled at this, and it seemed to him that Halli was as much fun as before.

Chapter 10--Halli and Queen Thora

In the spring King Harald went to the Gula Thing, and one day he asked Halli what he thought about women at the Thing. Halli answered:

Good is this, at the Gula Thing
We can seduce all we want.

The King went north to Trondheim, and as they rounded Cape Stad, Thjodolf and Halli were taking their turns at cooking. But Halli seemed seasick and lay down under the rowboat, and Thjodolf had to cook everything alone. While he was carrying the food, he fell over Halli's foot, which stuck out from under the dinghy. Then Thjodolf said this:

Under a boat a foot sticks out.
Are you making love?

Halli answered:

What I'm making, Thjodolf,
Is you to cook the meat!

The King kept on sailing until he came to Trondheim. The queen, Thora, was with him there, and she was little pleased with Halli. Still, the King liked him, and thought he was always fun to have around. One day, it was said, the King and his men went out in the street. Halli was with them. The King held a gold inlaid ax in his hand. Its shaft was wrapped in silver, and it had a large silver ring around the handle. At the bottom was a costly jewel. It was a worthy treasure. Halli looked at the ax all the time. The King saw this and asked if Halli really liked the ax. Halli said he did.

The King said, "Have you seen a better ax?"

"I don't think so," said Halli.

"Would you mount a man for the ax?" asked the King.

"No," said Halli, "but it's only fair that you should want to sell it for what you paid."

"And so it shall be, Halli," said the King, "take the ax and use it as the best of men. It was given to me, and so shall I part with it."

Halli thanked the King.

In the evening, when the men were drinking, the Queen spoke with the King. She said it was strange and most unfitting to give Halli that costly gift, and she added, "Such is hardly right for a low-born man to own--and for his foul insults! There are many who get less for good service to you."

The King said he would decide to whom he gave his treasures, and he added, "besides, I don't want to turn Halli's words, which could mean two things, to the worse."

The King asked that Halli be brought to him, and so it was done. Halli bowed to him. The King told Halli to say something that could mean two things for Queen Thora, and he added, "and let's see how she takes it."

Halli then bowed to Thora and said:

Most well-matched you are.
Of great note is it, Thora,
That into a steep crag you turn
The whole of Harald's cock.

"Take him and slay him!" said the Queen, "I don't wish to have his foul slander on me."

The King bade no one be so bold as to seize Halli for this, and he added,"Don't take this so hard, Thora. Do you think another woman would make a better bedmate and Queen for me? You scarcely know how to hear your own praise."

Skald Thjodolf had been in Iceland while Halli was away from Norway. When he got back, he brought with him a good horse, which he wanted to give to the King. The King looked at the horse. It was large and fat. Halli was there and saw the horse had its cock out. He said:

Lewd is the beast.
The cock of Thjodolf's horse
Tells me he must be
After a master.

"Gross!" said the King, "he'll never be owned by me!"

Halli remained one of the King's men, and one day asked the King's leave to go to Iceland. The King told him to go with care, because of Einar the Fly. Halli went to Iceland and settled there. But when his money had run out, he had to start rowing out to fish. One time he got caught in a tide so strong he almost didn't get back. In the evening, porridge was brought to him, and after he had eaten a few bites, he fell back and died.

Later, Harald learned of the death of two of his men out in Iceland, one Bolli the Proud, and Shuttle Halli. He said of Bolli, "Before a spear will this warrior have fallen." But of Halli he said, "Porridge killed the clown." I end there the saga of Shuttle Halli.

Notes on the Story of Shuttle Halli

[1]Magnus the Good ruled from 1035-47; Harald Sigurdson (Hard-Ruler) from 1047-1066. Magnus was Harald's nephew.

[2]Thjodolf Arnorson was attached first to the court of King Magnus, then later to Harald's court. Thjodolf served Harald through many campaigns, then fell with his King at the Battle of Stamford Bridge in 1066.

[3]This was a bell for the church built on the site of the Althing.

[4]The name is unknown; perhaps a troll or beast of some sort. The gibe is obscene.

[5]The incident referred to is related by Snorri in the _Skáldskaparmál_. Thor arrives at the hall of Geirrod, and Geirrod picks up a red-hot ingot and throws it at him. Thor catches it in midair with his iron gloves and throws it back. It goes through the pillar behind which Geirrod is hiding, through Geirrod, and through the wall.

[6]Byzantium.

[7]Probably a criticism of the King's cooks.

[8]A long lay with a refrain every two, three, or four stanzas. It was invariably heroic and laudatory in nature, though the form could conceivably be used to treat any subject.

[9]The incident here referred to is related in a short story called _Þorleifs þáttr jarlsskálds_ (The Story of Thorleif Jarl-Skald). In the story Thorleif has journeyed from Iceland to Norway to sell some wares. Jarl Hakon insists they all be sold to him. Thorleif refuses, and Hakon plunders the ship and kills the men. Thorleif goes to Denmark and wins the friendship of King Svein. He then returns to Norway disguised as an old man and composes a magical scoffing verse on Hakon. The verse causes violent itching on Hakon; his beard falls out and half his hair. All the weapons in the hall begin to act on their own and several of Hakon's men are slain by them. Victorious in his revenge, Thorleif returns to

King Svein who notes the disgrace caused by the verse will be long remembered, and he gives Thorleif his nickname, Thorleif Jarl-Skald.

[10]Harold Godwinson ruled England for a few months in 1066.

[11]The "southern men" were probably Germanic people from the continent.

[12]Apparently, the Danes had little reputation for the skaldic art. The names of no Danish skalds have survived.

THE STORY OF GOLD ASA-THORD

In the days of King Eystein, the son of Magnus Barelegs, a man called Thord came out from Iceland.[1] An East Fjord man by birth, he was poor but able, better in fact, than his father, and among his equals he held his own. He was also a good skald.

When he got to Nidaros he had little money left for food. In the evening he went to the house of a woman called Asa. She was a high-born woman and very wealthy. She was closely related to Vidkun Jonson and others from Bjarkey Island. She talked to Thord for a while. He amused her well, and she began to like him. He got her to keep him, and he stayed there as a close friend during the winter. His honor grew, the longer he stayed with her, and many said they were very close together. They spent long times talking only to each other. Asa was not a young woman.

During the spring she told Thord she was very fond of him and added, "I shall set you up with money for a trading voyage to England, and we'll share the profits." He was very successful on the trading trip, came home in autumn, and stayed there for the winter. As the next summer passed, their profits grew very large, and it seemed the longer he stayed with Asa, the more he prospered. He came to be called Gold Asa-Thord.

Asa's kinsmen thought not much honor came from her being with Thord and openly talked of their dislike. But Thord acted as if he hadn't heard. One day Asa had a talk with Thord and said, "My kinsman, Vidkun Jonson, wants to come here, and I want you to honor him greatly with your service. It also seems smart to me that you compose a praise poem about him and recite it before he leaves. Honor him greatly in your poem, for good praise is valued by most chieftains. Thus we must make it so it pleases him very well. Be careful to choose the right words. His friendship will be helpful to you no matter who you come up against here in Norway."

Thord said he would chance it, and he composed the poem.

Later on, Vidkun came with a great number of men and took lodging at an inn. One day Thord went to Vidkun, greeted him, and said, "I have brought a little poem that I've made for you, and I wish you would give it a hearing."

"So it shall be," said Vidkun, "You are the first to compose a poem about me, and you must make it so that the poem honors me -- only then will I listen. I do not love you as much as my kinswoman, Asa, does."

It was a _drápa_ with fifty verses and had this refrain:

> Most wise Vidkun Jonson,
> Ever in throng of battle,
> Always a hard battle-candle, (sword)
> Reddens with blood.

When the poem was done, many praised it-- Vidkun the most--and he quickly changed his mind about Thord. He gave him a gold ring that weighed a mark.[2] Thord said he didn't need money, that he only hoped for his friendship. This Vidkun promised, and he saw Thord out, giving him good gifts.

Some time passed, and one summer, when Thord came back from England, he sailed up into the Nid river. King Eystein was then staying in Nidaros and had many great men with him. Among them were Sigurd Hranason, Vidkun Jonson, and the richest man of all, but very arrogant, Ingimar from Ask. He had anchored in the harbor before Thord came. Men talked about Thord's anchoring there, and said it would be better to lie up in another place. Thord said there was nothing wrong with anchoring there and he did nothing about it. But later, while they were talking about this and unloading the ship, Thord could not find his bow tent. He then went over to Ingimar's ship and found there a servant who had the tent wrapped up under himself. Thord picked up the man and the tent, took them home, and set them down.

Soon this news came to Ingimar. He was greatly angered. He went to Thord's house and asked him to give up the man right away.

Thord said, "It would hardly be right to let a thief escape, even if he is your man."

Ingimar answered, "You shall not, Gold Asa-Thord, hold my man any longer, or do anything to the thief. I could hardly be called a landowner if I let you, a beggar, drag a man away from me."

Then Thord answered and said:

Now tries the fierce tyrant
Greatly me to scare.
A brash man of yours
Stole a tent from me.
Now, I'll never let,
Giver of dragon's lairs (gold)
A known thief free,
Though you think to change that.

Ingimar left then and was greatly angered. Asa then asked Thord to send for Vidkun and ask him to make good his promise of friendship and reward for the poem. "Because," she said, "It's a grave matter to anger Ingimar."

Thord did so, and Vidkun left at once, saying he had a debt to pay. He came to Thord's loft with a great body of men, and it wasn't long before they heard a great din. Ingimar had come. He told Thord to let the man loose or he would attack.

Vidkun spoke then and said, "It is most fitting that this case come before a lawman. Thord has done only what he had to when he bound up the thief, otherwise he himself would have deserved punishment."

Ingimar said, "I'll be damned![3] She stood alone, and now--Vidkun is here! It is surely more fitting that we stick together than it would be for you to hold with Thord, your kinsman. Indeed, do you mean to reward him for paltry praise poems when he starts to make lampoons about you?"

Ingimar turned away at once, and Vidkun said, "Now I will send for Sigurd Hranason, my friend, and ask him to come here. If he has any doubts, then have him remember who helped him the most when the Finns attacked his home on Bjarkey Island."

Then they went and delivered his message.

Sigurd thought it better that Vidkun challenge Ingimar alone. "Because," he said, "each of you think you're the stronger." They reminded him, then, of Vidkun's last words. Sigurd said, "It's true that no one helped me as well as he, and it seems best to go and stand with him. Let's go!"

They went to Thord's loft. Shortly they heard a crowd of men in the street. Ingimar's men had surrounded the building. Then all the men came into Thord's loft, and Ingimar said, "Now we shall search for the man, Vidkun, if he is not led forward--and the sooner the better!"

Then Sigurd said, "Let's act with reason, Ingimar. It's a great injustice if you break into our house and rob us of that which belongs in the keeping of the King. Men will think to get justice from you even though you might be a powerful man."

Ingimar said, "The cock is no better off, though a hen shield him. It's an even worse business when the two of you stand against me--and you're both noble landowners. I shall turn back once more, but I will come a third time!"

After that, Sigurd sent men to King Eystein and asked him to come. "Say to him," he said, "that I was the last to leave his father, out west in Ireland." They went and told the King Sigurd's words. He allowed as how it wasn't beyond the strength of two men of note to deal with Ingimar. Then they told the King everything Sigurd had said.

The King said, "If it matters to him that I come, then so be it." The King went with a great body of men to meet Sigurd. A little later Ingimar went to the loft. He had four hundred men now and was a bit more eager to attack, if they wouldn't let the thief loose.

Then the King spoke. "It ill befits you, Ingimar," he said, "to raise so great a tumult in the town, to raise up so many men to plunder in the land. We shall not yield untried!"

Ingimar said, "Bad iron, say old women, makes a weak knife, and it is now a grave matter that the King himself comes here to stand between us. I must back away even this time."

And so it happened.

Later the King called together a Thing, and the thief was led forward with the tent on his back. He was judged and then hung to death on a riverbank. The King said, "What do you think, Ingimar, the thief will get now?"

"I should think," said Ingimar, "that a man who is slain for little reason will get good things."

"No," said the King, "he shall get Hell."

Ingimar said, "Your hands are mislaid, King, when you further the lot of the Suetlander[4] and dishonor your own men. It also seems to me no one as yet has strength or courage enough to avenge your father who was slain in Ireland like a dog at a fresh corpse. I also think he will get Hell who fights for something he isn't bound to."

After that, Ingimar went to his ship, sailed east, and slew three of the King's men in Vik. Later he went south to Denmark to live.

It is said about Thord that he later married Asa with the consent of Vidkun and the King. He stayed in Norway to his dying day, and was thought to be the bravest of men. And here ends the story of Gold Asa-Thord.

Notes on The Story of Gold Asa-Thord

[1]Eystein ruled Norway from 1103 to 1122.

[2]Eight ounces.

[3]The literal proverbial phrase for which I have substituted "I'll be damned" is "Stick me in here, said the shovel."

[4]A term of derision often used of the Icelanders.

THE SAGA OF THE OATH-BOUND MEN

Chapter 1--Odd's Youth

Ofeig was a man who lived in Midfirth at Reykir.[1] He was Skidi's son, and his mother was Gunnlaug, the daughter of Ofeig from Skard. Ofeig was married. His wife was named Thorgerd, Vali's daughter. She was a high-born woman of great repute. Ofeig was a very wise and shrewd man. He owned a great deal of land but few goods, for he wasn't at ease in money matters, and yet he was generous to everyone. He was a Thingman of Styrmir Thorgeirson, from the Asgeirsa River. Styrmir was then the greatest chieftain in the north.

Ofeig and his wife had a son named Odd. He was quite handsome and well-brought up, but he was little loved by his father for he wouldn't work on the farm except when he wanted to. There was also a man named Vali brought up there. He was a promising young man and very well-liked.

When Odd was twelve it was said about him that there was no man in the north who was better skilled, yet, Ofeig, his father, was cold to him and loved him little. One day Odd came to speak to his father, told him he wanted to leave, and asked him for a money settlement.

"The way it is," said Odd, "you don't honor me and I'm not useful to your household."

Ofeig answered that he would give only as much money as he had earned, and thus Odd could see for himself how much help he was going to get from him. Odd said he couldn't support himself with that and ended the talk.

The next day Odd took a fishing line down from the wall, all the fishing gear and six yards of plain wool, and he left, without farewells to anyone. He went out to Vatnsness and fell in with a band of fishermen. He rented the things he needed from them. Since they knew he came from a good family and since he himself was well liked, they risked his buying everything on credit.

He was with them all that year, and it was said whatever fishing party Odd was with always had the better luck. When he was there three winters and three summers, he had made enough to pay back everyone and still have some goods left over. Odd was very friendly with his fellow fishermen, but all this while Odd never went to visit his father, and they both acted as if they weren't kinsmen.

Later on, he took his goods north to the Strands[2] and got himself a ferry. With this he carried goods to the north coast; wood, whalemeat, and fish. He did this for a while and made a great deal of money. He came there only twelve years old, but by now he was fifteen and he had made so much money that he paid off the debt on the ferry and started sailing every summer between Midfjord and the Strands. But finally he grew to dislike this business, so he bought some dried fish and went out trading. He did very well in this, made a lot of money, and men talked highly of him.

After doing this for a while, he decided to buy a trading ship and the greatest share in the cargo. He now went on trading trips and became a very wealthy man, well-known and close to noblemen, and highly thought of even outside the country. Soon he had two trading ships working for him and it was said there was no trader as rich as Odd.

He was also luckier than other men. He never went farther north than Eyjaford nor farther west than the Hvita River. Mostly, he just went to Hrutafjord.

Chapter 2--Ospak Joins Odd

One time he came to Hrutafjord and meant to stay the winter. His friends asked him to settle there and he did so. He bought land at Mel in Midfirth, built a farm there and lived there in great prosperity, no less so than when he was a sea trader. No man in the northlands was as rich as Odd. He had more money than most men and he always helped his neighbors, but he never gave help or comfort to Ofeig. He behaved as if he didn't even know him.

Odd then laid up with his ship at Hrutafjord, and it was said that now no man in Iceland was as rich as Odd. He was so rich he had more money than the church, which was then very wealthy in Iceland. He had great stores of gold and silver as well as livestock and land. Vali, his kinsman, stayed with him whether he was in Iceland or abroad.

A man named Glum lived in the north at Skridinsenni, between Bitrufjord and Kollafjord. His wife was Thordis, daughter of Asmund Gray Hair, sister of Grettir, and their son was named Ospak.[4] He was a large man, strong, and very overbearing, and soon busied himself with trading goods. One summer he came to Midfjord, sold his goods and after a while, in the autumn, rode up to Mel and met Odd. They greeted each other and traded the news.

Ospak said, "Well, Odd, there's good talk about you. You're greatly praised, and all those with you think themselves lucky. Now I wish that to happen to me and I want to settle here near you."

Odd said, "You aren't praised very much, nor are you much liked, and you look a bit shifty. "

Ospak answered, "Judge from what you see yourself and not from the stories of others. I'm not asking you to support me, I only want to live under you and then you can see how it goes."

Odd said, "Your kinsmen are proud people and since you're pressing this matter so firmly, you can stay here for the winter."

Ospak took this with thanks and later he went to Mel in the autumn. He became Odd's handyman. He was a faithful worker and he worked hard. Odd liked him very much.

The winter passed and the spring came. Odd asked him to stay on, for it seemed to Odd better that way. Ospak wanted to stay and busied himself about the farm as before. The farm did very well, and it seemed to everyone that no Icelander had a better farm than Odd. Men thought only one thing seemed to mar his honor--he wasn't a chieftain. It was then the custom either to found a new chieftainship or else buy one.[5] Odd bought one and easily gathered Thingmen because everyone was eager to be with him. Nothing else happened for a while.

Chapter 3--Ospak and the Chieftainship

Odd was very pleased with Ospak. He was a hard, steady worker and useful to the farm. Another winter passed and Odd was even more pleased with Ospak since he had taken care of more jobs. In the fall Ospak brought sheep home from the hills, and it was a good roundup. Odd prospered more than anyone. Ospak also owned some sheep and he was so careful with them that he lost none.

The winter passed, spring came, and Odd told his friends that he meant to go abroad during the summer. He said his kinsman, Vali, would take over the farm.

Vali answered, "That's too great a task. besides, the farm seems to succeed most when you yourself are here, and anyway, I want to go with you."

Odd then asked Ospak to take over the farm. Ospak said, "I haven't wit enough to be head of such a great business."

Then Odd pressed the matter and Ospak still refused, but he came around to Odd's wishes when he was promised Odd's backing and power too. Odd said that he had seen that Ospak could best safeguard his assets, and he asked him to handle the farm in such a way that he might become a great man from it, and well-liked. Ospak said it would be so. Then they ended their talk.

Odd got his ship ready and had many goods brought to it. News of this got about quickly and was much was talked about. Odd wasn't long in outfitting the ship, and when he was ready his men went with him to the ship. Vali was going to make the journey with him. Ospak walked with Odd longer than the others for he had much to talk about with him. When they were almost at the ship Odd said, "There's one thing still unsettled."

"What's that?" said Ospak.

"My chieftainship isn't looked after and I want to take it up."

Ospak said, "That wouldn't be right, and I can't do it. I've already taken more in hand than it's likely I'll handle well. Besides there's no one more fitted for this than your father, a most wise and trustworthy man."

Odd said he wouldn't put it in his father's hands and he told Ospak, "I want you to take it."

Ospak refused.

Odd then said that it would anger him if he didn't take it, and so Ospak took it. Odd then journeyed abroad, and his trip went well. Ospak went back to Mel, and there was much talk about this. Everyone thought Odd had given too much power to this man.

Ospak rode to the Thing in the summer and handled himself very well, doing all that he was bound to do by the law, and he rode home from the Thing with honor. He backed his Thingmen eagerly, and didn't allow their suits to lose. He was also good to all his neighbors, and the farm did no less well now than before. There was no shortage of work and the business went forward quite well. The summer passed and later he hallowed the local meeting and was able to do that without error.[6] In the autumn he went to the hills and made a good roundup. Not one sheep was missing, either his or Odd's.

Chapter 4--Vali's Death

It came to pass that in the autumn Ospak went north into Vididale to the household of a woman called Svala. He was treated well there. She was a fair woman and young, and she asked him to oversee her farm. She said, "I've heard that you're a good householder. " They both liked each other well, talked together, and looked lovingly on each other. It wasn't long before he asked her who was to decide her marriage.

She said, "No kinsman is closer to me than Thorarin the Wise, chieftain of Laxdale. He's the son of Ospak Hoskuldson, the son of Kolls, and his mother was Thorgerd, daughter of Egil Skalla-Grim, the son of Kvedulf."

Later, Ospak went to meet Thorarin and was greeted well by him. He then brought up this matter with him.

Thorarin said, "i don't yearn to have you as a kinsman by marriage. There's too much talk about your doings, and this marriage is not in my interests. But I also know I can't take half measures with you. If I don't bring her over here under me, You'll do as you please. Still, I don't mean to get bound up in this."

Ospak left and went to meet Svala. He told her what had happened, and they decided to follow their own counsel. She betrothed herself to him by her own act.[7] Afterwards, they held their wedding feast, and she went back to Mel and lived there with Ospak, though they kept the farm at Svalasted.

The winter passed and when the spring came Odd came out to Hrutafjord. He had fared well and made a lot of money. When he came home and looked over his business, it seemed to him well cared for and he was in good spirits.

One time in the summer Odd told Ospak it suited him to have the chieftainship back.

Ospak answered, "To be sure, that was the thing I was least eager to take over, because I was unable to handle it; yet, I have taken care of it."

Odd said, "I heard that you handled it cleverly and well."

Ospak said, "Still, I think it's most customary to return the chieftainship at a legal meeting, either a local one or the Thing."

Odd said that suited him well.

The summer wore on, and the morning of the district meeting Odd woke up, looked around, and saw few men in the hall. He sprang up quickly. Ospak was gone and many men with him. That seemed strange to Odd, but he said little about it and made ready to go to the meeting with his men. When they got there, the meeting had just been hallowed, and many men were were just about to leave. This seemed to Odd even stranger.[8] The men went home, and as the days passed, a coldness arose between Odd and Ospak. Odd thought that Ospak greedily wanted to get some honor for himself and was making more of himself than was fitting, and Odd didn't mean to reward him by letting him do so.

One day Odd was sitting across the table from Ospak when, all of a sudden, he leaped up with an ax in his hand and made for Ospak, telling him to offer his hand and give back the chieftainship.

Ospak said, "Since you're so earnest about it, you shall have it back, though you don't need to get it by force. Other ways would be more fitting since I've done so much for you." He then offered his hand and pledged back the chieftainship.

Odd said, "I also think you've already had such honor from all this that you've been paid enough for all you've done.

After that they became very unfriendly with one another, and the work on the farm began to suffer, but Odd behaved as though he didn't know. Then one day Ospak made ready to leave. He loaded his pack horse and went away, with his wife, and with no farewells to Odd. He went to Svalasted and lived there. Odd acted as if nothing had happened.

It was said that in the autumn when the men from Mel went to the hills for the sheep roundup, it was quite different from the last time. Now Odd was missing sixty of his best sheep, and the mountains were searched for them. This seemed strange to many, for Odd was usually luckier with his goods than other men. There were many guesses about it, whether the sheep had wandered into another district, or were lost in a storm, or whether it was by man's doing. The matter died out after a while but what it meant was still much talked about, especially since Odd wasn't missing any other kind of stock.

Odd was quite sad during the winter. His kinsman, Vali, asked why he was so glum. He said, "Is it that you take the loss of the sheep so greatly to heart? You don't have a great spirit if something like that upsets you."

Odd said, "That doesn't bother me. What's worse is that I don't know who stole them."

Vali said, "If that's what you think happened, who do you suspect?"

"It's no secret," said Odd, "that I think it was Ospak."

Vali said, "Your friendship has worsened since the time you made him foreman over your farm."

Odd said, "That was a blunder, even though things turned out better than I thought."

Vali said, "Many thought it a strange thing to do, but the way it is now, you shouldn't charge him so quickly, for it's said that your friendship has gone to pieces and men would see this as just bitterness on your part. Now let's get together on this. Let me take over, and I'll find out whether he stole the sheep or not."

Odd said, "How can you find that out?"

Vali answered, "I'll make as though I'm selling goods and travel widely all over the district, but I'll really seek out Ospak's home."

Odd said, "Go and do as you wish. It's easy enough to do, but I think the plan will come to no good."

Thus they agreed to do this.

Vali then made ready for the trip into the Vatnsdale and Langadale districts. He was very well received everywhere. One evening he came to Ospak's home, and Ospak greeted him well. Ospak seemed very happy. When Vali left the next day, Ospak rode with him out of the yard and asked how things were going with Odd. Vali said things were going well. Ospak spoke well of Odd and said he was a very bighearted man. Then he asked, "But hasn't he had some losses in the winter?"

Vali said that it was so.

"What is said about this?" said Ospak, "Odd is usually very lucky with sheep."

Vali said, "There are many guesses about it. Some think they've fallen into a pit. Some think they may have wandered into another district. Some think it may have been the work of men."

"Something very uncanny has happened," said Ospak.

"To be sure," said Vali, "uncanny and bad, and much is said about it."

"That's to be expected," said Ospak.

"The fact is," said Vali, "now that we're talking openly about this, that some think it's not unlikely that it was your doing. Men put these two things together--your angry parting with Odd and the missing sheep right afterwards."

Ospak said, "I didn't think you would say that, and if we weren't such great friends I would take dire revenge for this insult."

Vali said, "You don't need to deny it, Ospak. It's unlikely you'll be able to escape this charge, for I've looked over your farm and I've seen that you have more livestock than usual."

"This won't prove to be true," said Ospak, "and I can only guess what my enemies must be saying when my friends talk in such a way."

"For sure," said Vali, "but this isn't said to you out of hatred, for I've spoken against you only while we're alone. Now if you do as I wish and level with me, you won't have a heavy fall because I'll fix it up. I am selling my goods all over the district, and I'll tell everyone you've come into some money and bought the livestock. Thus no one will suspect you, and I'll fix it so no dishonor will come to you if you listen to my plan."

Ospak said he wouldn't go along with it.

"Then it will go badly," said Vali, and they parted.

Vali went home and Odd asked what he had found out, but Vali was silent about it.

"Surely," said Odd, "there's no need to hide it, and if you won't say whether the stock were there, then I know Ospak has stolen them."

The rest of the winter was quiet, and when spring and the Summons Days had come, Odd went with twenty men to within a short distance from Ospak's farm.

Then Vali said, "Now Odd, you must unsaddle your horses and rest. I'll ride to the house to meet Ospak and find out if he'll settle. This matter doesn't need a legal suit to solve it. You should remember your old friendship with the man."

"I don't know how pressing that is," said Odd.

Vali went at once to Svalasted. There were no men outside. The door stood open, and Vali went in. It was dark in the first room, and before he knew it a man leaped at him with an ax and struck him between the shoulders. It was Ospak.

Vali said, "You're a very unlucky man, for you've wounded an innocent man. Leave now and save yourself. Your slayer will catch you if you wait here. Odd is just outside the yard and he'll kill you. Save yourself by sending your wife to him. Have her tell him we made a settlement, and that I've gone about my business elsewhere in the district."

Then Ospak said, "This has been the worst of deeds. I meant it for Odd."

He sent his wife out to Odd, and she told him Ospak and Vali were agreed on a settlement, that Ospak had confessed, given him the power of judgment, and asked that Odd turn back. Odd did so and rode home to Mel. He believed what was said to him. The next day Odd saw a large number of men come into the yard at Mel. Odd went out among them and saw why. The men came with Vali's body. Then it all came out, and Odd learned what had happened. He took it poorly and mourned greatly, and he had his slain foster brother buried beside the yard.[9] Many thought ill of Odd. Ospak disappeared, and nothing was heard of him.

Chapter 5--Odd's Mistake

Odd made his case ready for the Thing and called up nine neighbors for judgment. Later, it was said one of the neighbors had died, so Odd called up another in his place. They went to the Thing, and there was honor in this since he had a most pressing need to pursue the matter of his foster brother. Odd pitched his booth. He had many men with him. When the time for judging came, Odd went to the court, pressed the charge, and then called the defense.

A short distance away sat Styrmir and Thorarin with their men. Styrmir said to Thorarin, "Do you hear now what's going on in this case of Ospak's?"

"I hear," he said.

"Well," said Styrmir, "will you take up the defense for Ospak?"

"No," said Thorarin, "I won't have anything to do with it. Odd is to be pitied and has just need to go after such a man. I don't think Ospak is a good man."

"True," said Styrmir, "the man isn't good, still, you're bound to him in one way."[10]

"Well," said Thorarin, "I don't care about that."

Styrmir said, "You should think of the trouble that may come if he's outlawed. But there's a way out of that since both of us can see a defense in this case. Odd has wrongly brought it forward. For the neighbor who died Odd called up another while he was still in the district. He was supposed to do that at the Thing, and that's a flaw in the case.

Thorarin said, "I've seen that for a long time, but so great does Odd's need for justice seem in this matter that I doubt if I have the heart to go against him."

Styrmir said, "It seems to me this case most belongs to you, and dishonor will come to you if you see a good defense and don't do anything about it. Besides, it's a good thing that Odd see there are more men of mark here in the north than just himself. He treads us underfoot and our men as well, and no one else is talked about. Because of this, he easily gathers Thingmen for himself and lessens our esteem."

Then he sprang up and went to the court and said, "Here are the men who will answer for Ospak, and you have wrongly brought the case forward. There's a flaw in it. You now have two choices. Either drop the case as it now is, or we shall go on with the defense and use this flaw which we know for sure is covered by the law." Then he told Odd what the flaw was.

Odd was sorrowed by this, for it seemed the matter had dishonored him. He left and went to his booth.

In the alley between the booths, a man waited. He was old and weak. He wore a black cape with one sleeve in it and carried a gnarled staff with a spike on top. It was Ofeig, Odd's father. He greeted Odd first and said, "Well, your case went swiftly. Surely you have been honored by the settlement. Is Ospak outlawed or not?"

Odd said, "Outlawed he should be!"

"Outlawed he should be?" said Ofeig, "is there any doubt about that? He was charged with killing your foster brother, Vali, and stealing from you. Didn't he do those things?"

Odd said, "No one denies that, but the case was flawed. It was wrongly brought forward."

Ofeig said, "How could there be a flaw in your case? That's hardly likely. But could it just be that you are unaware that you're cleverer at trade and profit than at law--that you thought yourself to know enough and didn't need to seek the counsel of other men? I knew you had wrongly brought the case forward, but you thought yourself too good to ask me. You value anyone before me, and I knew you would be dishonored by this."

Odd said, "You were right."

Ofeig said, "How would it be if I still wanted something to do with you? Would you spare some money if someone set things right?"

Odd answered, "I wouldn't be unwilling to pay to get rid of the shame that has come from it, but it seems strange that you will set it right because I've never gotten anything from you."

Ofeig said, "If you want, you may risk some money on this, although I would almost let you keep the shame that's come to you. How far had the case gotten when you left?"

Odd said, "The flaw hadn't been brought up as a defense when I left the court."

Ofeig said, "That is the one thing that will help us most in this case, and you did that unwittingly."

Chapter 6--Ofeig and the Judges

Odd stayed at the booth, but Ofeig went back to the assembly and came to the North Quarter court. He asked what was going on there and was told some cases had been settled and some were ready for summing up. Ofeig said, "Would you let me go before the court?"

That was granted him so he sat down and said, "What about Odd's case? Is Ospak outlawed or not?"

They answered that he wasn't.

Ofeig asked, "How can that be? Isn't there a crime in this? Didn't he kill Vali and steal as well?"

They answered, "No one denies this, and no one was happy with the matter, but there was a flaw in the case. It was wrongly prepared." Ofeig said, "How can any flaw be worth more than the crime itself? Were you under oath?"

They said they were.

Ofeig said, "I see, and how were you bound by that oath? Wasn't it like this--that you swore an oath to judge rightly and truly as well as in agreement with the law? You must have said that, and what is truer or righter than to judge this killer and thief, this worst of men, an outlaw without shelter? But you've judged only what was most in agreement with the law. That, above all, will bring ill will. Which has more worth, the one part that deals with following the law, or the other two. It seems wiser to me to take that choice which honors both God and men, which you have sworn to do, and bring judgment on the one who has done this. It's a grave thing to judge one free when outlawry was the fitting sentence, and men won't think well of this. I want to give an eighth mark of silver to those of you who sit in judgment and a half mark to the one who sums up the case, because there's most need in this case not to let a criminal get off who has slain an innocent man and is surely a thief.[11] I know there must now be talk about this, and I'll defend what I've said."

He fared so well in the talk that they asked him to judge the case, if Odd would come back. Odd was sent for, and he came to the court. By this time most of the men had gone back to their booths and didn't know about this. The case was judged, and they made Ospak an outlaw. They then went back to their booths and spent the night. In the morning they went to the Law Rock where Odd stood up and said, "The man called Ospak was outlawed in the night by the North Quarter court."

He then told whan Ospak looked like so that he might be easily known as an outlaw--and he did this very loudly!

Chapter 7--Styrmir Forms the Band

Now men thought this change in the case strange indeed. Styrmir started talking and said, "Do you hear Thorarin, what's being said?"

"I hear," said Thorarin.

Styrmir said, "We've come up against treachery, and there are clever men to deal with."

"That's so," said Thorarin, "but there's still some help in the oath they swore."

"How's that?" said Styrmir.

"They've brought money into the judgment, and a charge can be made against those who did it and those who took it."

Styrmir said, "Then there's hope we can right this case."

"It won't be done quickly," said Thorarin, "twelve months must pass first. Now we must meet with friends and kinsmen."

Then they went back to the booths and got these men together for a talk: First was Styrmir, himself, then Thorarin; the third was Hermund; the fourth Jarnskeggi, from Thvera River, son of Einar Eyjolfson; the fifth Skeggbroddi, from the east at Vapnafirth; the sixth, Gellir Thorkelson from Helgafell; the seventh, Egil Skulason, from Borg; the eighth, Thorgeir Haldorason, from Laugardale.

These eight men were bound together by kinship and brotherhood, and they began their talk. They excitedly talked over Thorarin's plan, and Styrmir and Thorarin egged them on by hinting that they might gain as much from it as Odd had done. There were some in this group who were short of money and really needed it, but there were also some who wanted money though they had a great deal already, and they all thought it only just to charge that Odd's money had been used as bribery in the case, so the chieftains all joined together to support each other in getting either outlawry for Odd, or self-judgment. All this was done in secret, and the men then went home from the Thing with Odd still having been honored by his case.

A year passed, and one day Odd was riding to the hot springs as he often did, when he met his father there, and things got better between them. Later in the spring when they met again, Ofeig said, "Have you heard anything new, Odd?"

He answered, "I have no news."

"I've heard," said Ofeig, "that Styrmir and Thorarin have gathered a band and mean to ride here to charge you with bribery last summer."

Odd said, "I don't think it's beyond my strength to handle the two of them."

Ofeig answered, "It's graver than that. Many men are bound up with them in this case," and he named them.

Odd was silent.

Ofeig asked, "What should we do now?"

Odd said, "Go to the Thing, give the chieftains money and get their support in this."

Ofeig answered, "That doesn't seem wise to me. No one may support you against these chieftains, and we alone aren't strong enough. It seems wiser for you to get your ship ready during the Thing, stock it well, and sail away to another land. Also, it's better to give me some money than to let them take it."

Odd said, "You shall get some money. I think it's better you have it."

Then they parted. Styrmir and Thorarin left to summon Odd, but they knew nothing about this. The case went to the Althing.

Chapter 8--Ofeig at the Thing

Odd got ready for his journey while the chieftains rode north. Ofeig rode with Styrmir and Thorarin. They met Hermund with his men at Blaskogi moor, also Egil and Gellir, then they all rode south on the moor. Skeggbroddi, Jarnskeggi, and Thorgeir Haldorason rode from the East Fjords and met them at Reydarmuli. The whole band met together on the fields above the booths, and they all rode together to the Thing.

There was much talk about this case. Everyone now thought Odd would be beaten, with all these chieftains against him, and many were also vexed that he was so overwhelmed.

One day after the start of the Thing, Ofeig left his booth and went to the booth of the Myra men. Egil was outside, busy talking with someone. Ofeig waited, and when Egil turned to go back inside, Ofeig grabbed him by his coat and greeted him. Egil returned the greeting.

Then Ofeig said, "I wish you would sit down and talk with me."

Egil said, "You'll be wanting to talk about the case of your son, Odd, but there's no need to talk about that because it's lost already, and besides, Hermund and Styrmir have more say in this than I."

Ofeig said, "Ill find more amusing things to talk about than Odd's case. Besides, it's good just to talk to you."

Egil said, "I won't refuse to talk to you," and he sat down.

Ofeig said, "Are you a landholder, Egil?"

"That's true," he said.

"Do you live at Borg in Borgarfirth?" said Ofeig.

"I live there," said Egil.

"Good things have been said about you," said Ofeig, "that you're a great man, brave and generous. Some men even say that we are somewhat alike--not rich, but always willing to help our friends."

Egil said, "It pleases me to be thought like you, but while we're talking about who's rich and who isn't, how rich a man is Odd? You surely know."

Ofeig said, "But you said there was no need to talk of that matter. Of course I know how much money he has. It's more than anyone thinks. Are you a bit curious about the size of your share?"

"Very much so," said Egil, "and you're a good fellow."

"I think," said Ofeig, "that your share will be a sixteenth part of the Mel lands."

Egil said, "Then it doesn't seem to me that he's as rich as you say."

Ofeig said, "It isn't that. He doesn't lack riches. It's due to the way his goods and land will be divided. When you began the suit, didn't you all agree that you would get half the estate and the district men the other half, as the law says? Well then, as I see it, since there are eight of you, you should get a sixteenth part of the Mel lands. Besides that, did you really think Odd would sit quietly through all this while you take it to the Thing? By now he will be at sea with all his goods but the land, and I think the ship will sail under him even though you have done worse things to him than the court will see. He knows the sea passage to Borg isn't all that long, should he want to come to Bogarfjord--and there he would find you home! So also would he find Gellir's home at Helgafel if he went to Breidafjord, and if he should go north, it may come into his mind that he wouldn't be far from Thvera if he went as far as Eyjafjord, and if he went to Vapnafirth, he knows he would find the homestead at Hof. He could also go away, and I should think he would be welcome in other lands since you've been so unjust to him here. You'll get from all this only what you deserve, no money and your share of dishonor."

Egil answered, "It must be true that Odd isn't going to sit still, and there is one man in this case I would like to see come off badly. That's Hermund from Gilsbakka. He has behaved badly with us for a long time."

While they talked about this Ofeig let a moneybag slide down from under his cape. Egil followed it with his eyes. When Ofeig saw Egil looking, he pulled it back up under the cape. He said to Egil, "Are you thinking of something else?"

"Oh no," said Egil.

"No?" said Ofeig, "that was no illusion. You saw what you lack," and he unwound the moneybag, poured the silver out on his lap, picked some up in his hands, and showed it to Egil. He said, "Here are two hundred ounces of silver that I want you to have for not going against us in this case--for I would bestow on you alone, of all those who have a part in this, a good fortune from it. Also I know that you're wise enough to see that it's better to take this honor from me than to get nothing from it at all, as the others will."

Egil said, "I think you're the worst of men. Do you think I'll break my oath for your bribe?"

Ofeig said, "I didn't ask you to break your oath. Didn't you all swear you would get either outlawry for Odd or self-judgment? Now it may come to pass in this case that we kinsmen would allow your band to take self-judgment. Further, if it should so happen that you're the one to assess, surely you don't have to answer to anyone for how much you fine--or how little. Thus you can bring about an honorable settlement and keep your oath as well--and also have my thanks."

Egil said, "You're a very sly man, and it could indeed turn out as you say, but I don't have the heart to go against all of them alone."

Ofeig said, "Well, if I got another to come into it with you, would you take it up then?"

Egil said, "That would be better."

Ofeig said, "Just suppose that I could choose any of them--though I wish all of them ill but you."

Egil said, "There are two. One is Hermund, he is closest to me in kinship, but I wouldn't choose him. The other is Gellir Thorkelson. I'd choose him for this."

Ofeig said, "Good, I'll go find him, and I'll tell you what happens, but you keep the money."

"So be it," said Egil, and they parted.

Chapter 9--Gellir Joins Up

Ofeig went to Gellir's booth and called him. He came out. Ofeig humbly greeted him and asked to talk with him. Gellir said, "I think you will want to talk about Odd's case."

"Hardly," said Ofeig, "I think there are many more tempting and amusing things to talk about than Odd's case. I enjoy more just talking to wise men, and it's said that you are wise."

Gellir said, "I won't deny you a visit, Ofeig."

Then they sat down.

Ofeig said, "Which of the men in the west seems to you most likely to become a chieftain."

Gellir answered, "There are many. I would name first the sons of the chieftain, Snorri, or the sons of Thorgil Arason, or the Eyramen, sons of Steinthor."

"Indeed," said Ofeig, "I've heard about the same thing, but which of the daughters seem to you the best matches?"

Gellir said, "I think the same families. I would say the daughters of Snorri, or Thorgil Arason, or Steinthor. These are the women with the most honor."

Ofeig said, "Do you have any daughters?"

"I have," said Gellir.

"Are they married?"

"No," said Gellir.

"Why is that?" said Ofeig.

"Because," said Gellir, "no rich, landed men of high birth have come by. I'm not a rich man and can't give dowries great enough. But now let me ask you a question. Who are the men in the north that seem to you most likely to become chieftains?"

"Well," said Ofeig, "there are many. I would say first Einar Jarnskeggjason, or Hall, son of Styrmir from Asgeirsa River. Some say my son Odd should be counted with the men of note--and now I must give you the message which Odd asked me to give if I found you--that he wants to marry Ragnheid, ycur daughter. Also, here are four hundred ounces of silver by which he takes care of the dowry. Now think! Who would ever make an offer such as this, not cnly to take care of the dowry himself, but also to provide for you as long as you live?"

Gellir said, "I wouldn't have denied him before, but as things stand now, I shouldn't let him while this case, which now is greatly talked about, hangs in the balance."

Ofeig said, "Don't you think that business is madness?"

Gellir said, "I don't know if your offer is any better. I've prayed and wished for the suit to win, but I've not been so eager for the match."

Ofeig said, "You're to be pitied if you think you can solve your money problems with a share in the judgment against Odd."

"Nonetheless," said Gellir, "we think so."

Ofeig said, "Are you curious how much your share would be?"

"Very much so," said Gellir, "tell me."

Ofeig said, "To the eight of you will be given half the Mel lands, but you'll get more hope from this than riches, for Odd will be at sea, and he'll be welcomed in other lands while you stay here with your dishonor."

Gellir said, "You're cunning, and that may be true, but in some ways it's not all that bad."

Ofeig said, "He said he just might go looking for your farm if he came to Breidafjord, and if he did, you wouldn't find entrance easy when you came home!"

Gellir said, "I'm not afraid of that."

"But you must see," said Ofeig, "how this case will turn out for you. You'll get neither honor nor money, but only the things I've just told you. I want you to take the money. Think how little your share is, or anyone else's, in this case. I also tell you that you'll never lack for money while you both live. You'll have the worthiest kinsmen and not have to pay the dowry."

Gellir said, "What you're saying is true, and I can see now I won't gain from the case, but never have I been known to be a traitor. I've sworn an oath to the others that we must end the case with either outlawry for Odd or self-judgment."

Ofeig said, "I didn't ask you to break your oath. It may happen that the case will come under you and we kinsmen decide to yield you self-judgment. Then it could happen that you won't be so wicked as to make us pay up more than we're able, and then Odd won't be outlawed. So, if the case comes under you and if all happens in this way, then you won't be dishonored. You kept your oath and showed heart, and you can have this money and do well by your daughter."

Gellir said, "You're a wise man, but I don't have the heart to go alone against the others, even though I have a mind to."

Ofeig said, "How would it be if I brought others into this?"

"That would help," said Gellir.

"Who would you pick for this," said Ofeig, "just suppose I had the choice of any."

"I would pick Egil for it," said Gellir.

Ofeig said, "I see. You pick the worst man for this. I guess you don't care who profits from it. But at least he's smart enough to know it's better to have some honor than none."

Gellir said, "I will do it, if you bring him into it."

Ofeig said, "Now I'll go find Egil, and if he goes along with it, then you must talk it over with him beside the church. If your men stand around nearby, no one will think it strange you're talking together. You can then make a plan together."

They parted then, and Ofeig found Egil and things went as Ofeig had foreseen.

Chapter 10--The Judgment

The next day Ofeig went over the bridge to see his kinsmen the Skardamen and asked them to go with him to the Law Rock. They did so, and when his case was brought up, Ofeig stood up and said, "I haven't said much about my son Odd's case, but now I wish to get a settlement for it."

Hermund said, "There'll be no settlement for this."

Ofeig answered, "Then this could be a short case, but are you saying that kinsmen don't have the right to choose terms in this, either outlawry or self-judgment?"

Hermund said, "You can choose if you want, but only self-judgment. To outlaw is not in your power."

Ofeig said, "Well, can kinsmen still pick who they want from your band of judges, or are you going to make all the rules?"

Hermund said, "You can pick who you want. We haven't the power of choice."

Ofeig said, "Fair enough, we won't choose outlawry. We agree to that, as you wanted, but you must now drop the case at law, and I'll pick men from your band who I think are fit for this, one, or two, or more."

Hermund said, "Let it be so."

Thorarin the Wise said, "Agree today only to what we won't regret tomorrow!"

Hermund said, "We will agree to this."

"Shake hands on it," said Ofeig, and so it was done, and they dropped the case at law.

Ofeig then gave money as surety for any fines awarded by the men he chose as judges. Afterwards Ofeig said, "Now let's go up to the Thing Plain, and there I'll choose for this those I find fitting." They did so, and a great crowd thronged up to the field, and Gellir and Egil came also with their men. The Ofeig said, "The eight of you sit down in a ring, and I'll come before you and choose those for my case whom I think fitting." They all sat down, and Ofeig went first to Styrmir.

He knelt down, pushed back the hood of his cape, and said, "Everyone must think that I'll choose you for my case since I'm your Thingman and have given you good gifts. It would seem likely that the case was well-placed if you handled it. But no one has been as zealous in this as you. This case has brought more sorrow than joy to my son Odd, and the start of it was all your doing, so I'll keep you out of it."

"There you sit, Thorarin. It's not that you're too short of wit to handle this case, but it's that you've used all the wit you have to bring trouble to my son, so I'll keep you out of it."

"There you sit, Hermund, a great chieftain."

At this Hermund greatly puffed himself up and thought he would surely be chosen.

"Everyone now knows," said Ofeig, "that you have taken this up only out of greed, wickedness, and injustice, and no one has been as eager about it as you. Also, you don't need the money, and have only done it for the esteem it might bring. Thus, I'll keep you out of it."

"There you sit Jarnskeggi. I'm told you carried a banner before you at the Vadla Thing in the north, as though you were a king, and I can only guess how much your pride would grow if you got honor from this. So I'll keep you out of it and make sure that for your part you'll get no honor from this."

"There you sit, Skeggbroddi. Didn't I hear that King Harald said you were the best fitted for Kingship of all the men in Iceland?"[12]

Skeggbroddi said, "I don't know about that. King Harald said much like that to me, but I don't know how much he meant it."

Ofeig said, "Even less than I agree to your being King of Iceland do I agree to your being king over this case, so I'll keep you out of it."

"There you sit, Gellir. You're said to be a good chieftain and just, though you've not been noble in this. Yet there's some excuse for you in that you're short of money and your good friend Skeggbroddi is in it too. Also, it seems to me, of all of them your part is the smallest--and the case does have to go to someone--well, I won't choose you for it, but I won't keep you out of it either."

"There you sit Thorgeir. I make only a short stop here, because you've never before handled anyone's case--you haven't the wit for it."

When Ofeig came before Egil he looked around, tugged at his cape hood, and said, "I think I've shared the fate of wolves--who don't know they've eaten each other up until they come to the tail. So it is with me. I've gone before many noble men to choose someone for my case, but now the only one left is one whom everyone knows doesn't care how he gets his money--and that's Egil. I must now either go back and choose one of those I set aside, or choose you, whom everyone knows won't do well by me. Still, I think it wise to choose you for this."

Egil sprang up and said, "Very often honor will come to us though others don't want it to. Let's go Gellir, and think over the case."

They went away and Egil said, "What should we do? I think we should fine lightly. But that surely won't help the others."

"Their hatred will fall on us," said Gellir, "how lightly should we fine?"

Egil said, "We'll fine thirteen ounces of silver."

Gellir said, "I'm not eager to tell the sentence."

"Would you rather tell the sentence," said Egil, "or sit for the reply?"

"No," said Gellir, "I'll tell the sentence--you sit for the reply!"

They got up and went back.

Hermund stood up and said, "Let's all listen to Odd's disgrace!"

Then Gellir said, "We mean to fine Odd thirteen ounces of silver."

Hermund said, "Did I hear you right--that you fined him thirteen hundred ounces of silver?"

"I'm sure," said Egil, "that you weren't sitting on your ear when you stood up. I said thirteen ounces of silver, and only such silver as the poor would take in payment, broken rings and trinkets."

Then Hermund said, "We're betrayed!"

Egil said, "Do you really think so?"

"For sure," said Hermund, "I think so, and you have betrayed us, traitor!"

Egil said, "Then I do only what seems best--to betray one who trusts in no one. You trust no man--friends, kinsmen, children or wife--not even yourself! Once you hid your money in such a great fog that you knew you'd never find it again even if you wanted to."

Hermund answered, "You're lying in this as you've done many times before. You always lie! The summer before last I asked you and the seven in your family to come from your wretched farm and stay with me at Gilsbakka. When you went home, you said thirty abandoned horses of mine had died and all had been eaten."[13]

Egil said, "One couldn't say too much about your thriftlessness, but I think little or nothing was eaten of them."

Hermund said, "I hope we don't meet at the Thing next time!"

Egil said, "Now I'll say something I thought I'd never say. You've finally said something of value. Long ago it was foretold that I should live to be the oldest of men, thus, if we're not both at the Thing next time, you must have been carried off by trolls!"

Then Styrmir said, "It's only natural that we fare poorly when we take the worst man around into our band. Egil is the worst man in Iceland and everyone knows it."

Egil answered, "It's only fitting that you call me the worst man around since everyone knows how many times you've said I was your equal! Now I'll tell of some great wickedness about you which others don't know about. When from looking at your own self-worth, you decide to take the worst man as an equal, you should also know that we're different in some ways too. You're a great eater, but stingy, and you have a jug which you call Lucky Food, and no one who visits you ever knows what's in it, no one but you. It's also known by others that you run away when the black handled battle-ax comes aloft, but I risk helping my friends, and I am generous with food. In these ways are we quite unalike."

Then Thorarin tried to stand up. He was very fat and heavy and had to steady himself with his hands on his knees. Egil said, "Sit back down, Thorarin, any answer I would give you is sure to make the whole Thing laugh at you." He sat down.

Then Egil said, "Now you do wisely--as it usual with you. It doesn't seem funny to me, though boys laugh at it, that you always sit scrunched up next to the fire rubbing your arms together."

Then Thorgeir said, "It's foolish to fine only thirteen ounces of silver."

Egil answered, "Well, it should seem especially wise to you! Don't you remember when you were east at the Arness district meeting and got hit on the head? You were struck by some houseboy, and thirteen bumps came up on your head, and you accepted as settlement a lamb for each bump."

Then Skeggbroddi said, "Jarnskeggi, let's leave--before he talks to us!" and they left.

Soon nearly everyone had gone away, but the money stayed where it was. No one wanted to take it. There was much ill will among them, and so ended the Thing.

Chapter 11--Odd Marries

Ofeig rode north to find his son, Odd. He was then ready to put to sea. He asked how the case had gone.

"I gave them self-judgment," said Ofeig.

"You rascal, you gave up the case," said Odd.

"Don't judge so quickly, kinsman," said Ofeig, and he then told him all about it.

Odd said, "I didn't think it would happen this way, and I shall reward you handsomely."

Ofeig said, "Your wedding shall be in six weeks, here at Mel."

Odd said, "That is chosen for me what I'd rather choose myself. I'm going on with my journey now to see how well I can do, but I'll come back after a while."

Ofeig said, "I don't know how to stop you. May you have good luck."

Odd sailed north with a fair wind to Thorgeirsfjord. Then the wind died, and he lay there a few nights. In front of them was a trading ship. Odd became restless there and had himself rowed to the land in a small boat. He went up a high mountain and saw the wind was blowing further out, though it was calm in the fjord. The men in the trading ship said he would need a lot of men to row across the sea.

Odd said, "If you think it madness to row, then you should wait here."

They found the breeze and didn't take down the sail until they reached the Orkneys. They stayed there a few weeks. When they went back later, with a good wind, the trading ship still lay there.

Odd sailed north and didn't stop until he reached Midfirth. He went home to his farm and made ready a great wedding feast, skimping on nothing for it.

Gellir came with his daughter, and then Egil and his men. The feast went as all had hoped, but Egil was not in good spirits. Odd sent everyone away with good gifts, but Ofeig said, "I wish that you would send Egil away handsomely. We must reward him well."

Odd said, "I thought you rewarded him before."

Ofeig said, "Not so, do a good honor to him."

The next day Odd said to Egil, "I had forty sheep and two oxen driven up to Hrutafjord, and by now they'll be at your home, and I'll never treat you meanly while we both live."

Egil thanked him, and his spirits rose. Gellir got great gifts along with Egil, and there they parted.

Chapter 12--Hermund and Ospak

The winter came and when it settled in, Hermund went to the Hvamm Thing. When he decided to go back, he told his men they should turn south to Borg and burn Egil in his house. But when they came out into Valfell, it seemed to them as if a string twanged up in the mountain pass, and right after this Hermund found he had a terrible pain under his arm. They turned home to find help for him. The pain got worse, and Hermund got sicker the longer they traveled. When they got to Hoggvandasted, the roof was all covered with ravens.

When they got home, Hermund was lifted into bed and Thord Solvason, priest at Rekjaholt, was sent for. When he came, Hermund couldn't speak so the priest went to his horse. They ran after him, and he came back again, but still Hermund couldn't talk. So the priest left and went down the glen, but they ran after him a third time. This time the priest stooped over Hermund and heard him whisper, "Five in the glen, five in the glen. . . "[14] Then Hermund died.

It is said that a man named Mar married Svala and took over the farm. Olvir, his brother, was a simpleton. Early one morning while Mar and Svala lay in bed, a large man came in and spoke a verse:

From its sheath I draw
A short, sharp sword.
Swiftly I thrust it
Into the body of Mar.
I hated to grant
To the offspring of Hildir
The warm embraces
Of Svala the fair.

He then stabbed Mar, but when he tried to leave, Olvir leaped up and stabbed him with a great knife.

Some time later men found twelve cattle put to death on the farm of the man who summed up the case against Ospak. Seven of Odd Ofeigson's stud horses were also slain. Still later Ospak was found dead beside a cave in Linakradale. There was a hand bowl beside him with dried blood in it. The wound and hunger had killed him.

Odd remained a powerful man. He had a son and named him Ofeig. Snorri Kalfson and the Midfirth men are descended from him, and here ends this saga.

Notes on the Saga of the Oath-Bound Men

[1]The action of this saga centers about Mel, located inland from Midfirth, on the northeast coast of Iceland.

[2]Horn Strands, on the extreme northeast peninsula, a distance of about a hundred miles from Midfirth.

[3]Eyjafjord is centered on the north coast, about a hundred miles west of Midfirth. The Hvita River, or Bogarfjord, is on the west coast, about thirty miles north of Reykjavik. Hrutafjord is the next fjord to the west of Midfirth.

[4]The "Grettir" referred to here is the famous Grettir Asmundarson, whose life is chronicled in Grettir's Saga one of the major Family Sagas.

[5]The authority of a chieftain was vested in a "goðorð" or mandate which the chieftain held while he lived, and which he could pass on to his heirs when he died. The mandate itself could be sold or bought. It could also be given away, owned in common by two or more chieftains, or even temporarily transfered (as later happens in this saga).

[6]It was customary to open a meeting by performing sacred rites to sanctify it.

[7]Self-betrothal was very unusual. Marriages were customarily arranged by the fathers involved or the nearest male kinsman.

[8]The hallowing of a meeting was the first order of business. That the men are preparing to leave apparently shortly after the hallowing is most unusual, and against the law which stipulated the meeting must last at least one day. Probably Ospak is bending the law and trying to conclude the meeting before the arrival of Odd since he, no doubt, will demand the formal return of the chieftainship.

[9]The practice of fostering is common in the sagas. The relationship was always a close one, and the death of a foster brother demanded revenge or compensation.

[10]According to Svala, Ospak's wife, "No kinsman is closer to me than Thorarin the Wise, chieftain of Laxdale" (155), thus there is an onus on Thorarin to help Ospak, even though he refused to support their marriage.

[11]A mark equaled eight ounces of silver.

[12]Harald Sigurdson (Hard-Ruler).

[13]To use otherwise useless horses for food implied an impoverished condition. The practice of eating horseflesh was later prohobited.

[14]In the *Möðruvallabók* version of the saga, Hermund sayd there are two hundred in the glen.

THE STORY OF GISL ILLUGASON

Chapter 1--Gisl's Plan

In the days of King Magnus, a man called Gisl left Iceland for Norway.[1] He was the son of Illugi Thorvaldson, the son of Tind. Tind was the brother of Illugi the Black. Gisl was seventeen years old when he went to Norway. He had been unhappy for a long time and he kept mostly to himself. He took up lodging in Forbodi with a rich man called Hakon.

Gisl took little interest in things during that winter and he was never cheerful. One time Hakon said to him, "I have thought about your nature, and it seems to me that you always have a very grave face. It must be either that you are getting ready for some great undertakings or that great things are bothering you. Now tell me what you're brooding over, and even though you should have great things to speak of, I shall not reveal them. But if you won't tell me, and go off from here and do grave deeds, that will little please me."

Gisl answered, "You guessed right, and I shall tell you the truth about it. There's a man called Gjafvald who now, I've been told, may be one of the King's men. This man struck my father and gave him his deathwound, so I've looked for him and his kinsman, Thormod Kollason, throughout Iceland, and now I've come to Norway. I mean to avenge my father or die here."

"That plan is not very promising," said Hakon, "because Gjavald is very close to King Magnus, and it won't be easy for a stranger to get him. Still, I won't deny you help in this."

King Magnus spent that winter in Nidaros and Gjafvald with him, well-honored. Gisl journeyed to the town and on the advice of Hakon, his landlord, tried this scheme. He had hot wax spilled on his face and he let it harden there. He was then not a very healthy sight.[2] He watched for a chance to get Gjafvald, but that chance wasn't easy to come by.

Chapter 2--Gisl's Revenge

One Saturday, early in the day, Gisl stopped in the street when he heard a great din. He saw it was King Magnus with a great body of men. He saw Gjafvald there. Just then a woman went out of one of the buildings. She had a child in her arms. It was Helga, Thormod's daughter, Gjafvald's wife. She called to her husband, and he went to meet her. The King and his company moved on.

When Gjafvald turned again down the street, there was only one other man with him. This time Gisl turned and struck him. The blow hit the shoulder joint, and the arm fell down but not all the way off. Gjafvald turned to face him. Gisl then hacked at the other shoulder joint, and this stroke was better than the first. Gjafvald fell.

Gisl leaped down to a gangway where a small boat loaded with firewood floated. An Icelander called Thorstein, a very small man, owned this boat. Gisl leaped out into the boat with Thorstein and together they threw the firewood overboard. Then he rowed over towards Bakki. When they got to the middle of the river, Gisl stood up and called back to the gangway. "If from that wound," he said, "which Gjafvald, one of King Magnus' men, has gotten--if from that battle-wound a slaying results, then I make known it was by my hand. I am called Vigfuss in the morning, but in the evening I believe I'm called Ofeig."[3]

Later on they landed up from Bakki, and Gisl jumped ashore there. By then the town was alarmed and the search begun for the men both by ship and on land. He was found in some brushwood and brought to the town. The King's men saw that Thorstein was the one who had carried Gisl across the river and they charged him with it. They said he would also die.

Then Gisl said, "Don't blame him for this. He couldn't stop me."

Gisl grabbed Thorstein when he got close to him. Thorstein was so little that he scarcely came up to Gisl's armpit. Gisl yanked him up off the ground with the other hand and said, "Now look at him. How could this puny wretch guard the boat from me if I wished to take it? I can throw him about like a child. Let him go in peace, because he is guiltless."

They did so and said that Gisl had spoken well and nobly. Gisl was put in those irons which King Harald Sigurdson had made and from which no man ever escaped. He had only the floor to sit on, and a woman kept watch over him.

At this time there were a great many men in the town. There were three Icelandic ships. Teit, son of Bishop Gizur, was master of one ship. Also there at that time was the priest Jon Ogmundarscn who later became the bishop at Holar.[4] Altogether there were no less than three hundred and sixty Icelanders in the town.

King Magnus was furious. He sat in judgment, and the town bishop was with him. The priest Jon was also there. He was a friend of the bishop. The King bade the man be slain, and at that moment the Nones bell rang.

The King said, "Is it now Nones? Look at the sun."

So it was done, and the nones had just begun.

Then the bishop said, "Lord, the man has the right to holy day peace, even though he greatly deserves his fate."[5]

The King said, "This is a trick of yours. You are scheming against me."

"That is not so, lord," said the bishop, "but you handle this as most agrees with you."

Later on the Icelanders bedded down together. There were many kinsmen and friends of Gisl, and they talked about the case and what courses they might follow. It seemed to them the case was not at all simple, and they didn't come to any agreement.

Chapter 3--Gjafvald's Last Words

Sunday came and word was sent to the King that Gjafvald wished to meet with him. The King went and met with him. Gjafvald said, "I wish now to set my estate in order, since it is not known how long a time I have left. I also wish to ask that you spare Gisl, because he bravely has avenged his father."

"That is not likely," said the King.

Gjafvald said, "You know, my King, that for a very long time I have been your follower, and I have taken great pains to shield your life with mine. I have been ready for anything you wished to set before me, whether for good or ill, but now I know that this may be the last of our meetings. I have now spoken with the priests, told them of my wishes, and taken last rites. They said to me that I would be saved if I now forgave that which was done against me. I hope, lord, that you should not in this way keep me from heaven's kingdom, and I being now doomed to die."

"May you have the best," said the King.

He went away, and Gjafvald died a little later.

Chapter 4--Gisl's Rescue

Early on Monday eight Icelanders met together, and Teit said, "Things will not have turned out well in our case here if our fellow countryman and highly esteemed brother-in-arms is slain. However, we can all see what great problems joining this case can bring since our lives and wealth are at stake. Now I put this forward as a plan--that we allow the judgment of the King, but if it does not happen that Gisl is to keep his life, then we shall either win this case ourselves or be slain for it, and in this we must support whoever becomes our leader."

They all said they wanted him to be leader and they wanted to follow his plan.

He said, "Then you should all plan to swear an oath to me that you will spare neither your lives nor your wealth in this, however I choose to go about the matter."

That they did. After that they took their bath, and just then a horn was sounded. Teit ran from the bath at once. He had on a shirt and linen pants and he wore a gold lace band around his forehead. Over him was a scarlet cloak that was brown on the inside and trimmed on the outside with gray fir. All the Icelanders were together there, but when the horn was sounded, they didn't all go right away to the meeting.

Teit said to them, "Let's move before the King's men do, and go at once to the room where Gisl is."

They went quickly down the street and made a great din. The woman opened the front window of the house. She ran into the room where Gisl was and said to him, "It's great bad luck for you to be down here, because now the King's men are on their way here."

Gisl answered, "Let us not grieve, foster-mother."

Then he made this verse:

Happy still shall I be,
Though warriors mean to kill the skald,
And the fetters' iron
Burns through to my bones.
Each man has to die, woman,
But a warrior's heart was shaped for me,
And proudly shall my prowess
Be in song still remembered.

The next moment they broke through the door, and it burst with a loud noise. The men saw that Gisl was startled only a tiny bit. Teit struck the fetters from him and took him into his band. They went in this way to the meeting.

Later Soni, the head of the King's men, came to the meeting from a different direction. He had meant to fetch Gisl. He said, "You didn't waste any time in this, Icelanders, but I think you gave heed only to your judgment about the man and not the King's. It is sure that you won't be forgetting what you have done this morning, for King Magnus has been angered by lesser offenses than the slaying of one of his bodyguards by the suet-devils!"[6]

Chapter 5--Gisl at the Thing

When the Thing had begun, Sigurd Wool-Rope stood up and said, "I think that most men must know that our fellow warrior, Gjafvald, is slain. A man came out from Iceland who thought he had a case against him. He intended at once to give Gjafvald a mortal wound rather than seeking a settlement, as is customary with other men. It would seem to us, the King's men, that it is but a little matter to pick off the King's bodyguard, one by one, and should this onslaught go on, the whole bodyguard. It may even be that they would all attack its head, and not respect the King any more than other men. Now there are such great shames worthy of great punishments that there would be no redress though ten Icelanders were slain for one of ours, in punishing them so for their foolhardiness in taking Gisl away from the King."

Then he stopped speaking. Teit Bishopson stood up and said, "Does the King wish to allow me to speak in this matter?"

The King asked the man who stood beside him. "Who is that man?"

He answered, "Lord, that is Teit Bishopson."

The King said to Teit, "By no means shall I let you speak, because all that you would say will do great harm. It would be only fitting if your tongue were cut out."

Then the priest, Jon Ogmundarson, stood up and spoke, "Will the King allow me to say something?"

The King asked, "Who speaks now?"

The man beside him answered, "The Icelandic priest called Jon."

The King said, "I will allow you to speak."

Then Jon put forth his case: "God is to thank that the lands have become Christian, Norway and Iceland, because before, men and the devil went forth together, but now the devil walks not so boldly in the sight of men. Now he gets men to carry out his business, and it is shameful to see that these words which have just been spoken are from the mouth of the devil. First is one man slain, and then he urges that ten should be killed. I think that such men work most out of wickedness and evil to desert mercy and righteousness and other good qualities of chieftains so to exhort men and sharpen their fierceness and wickedness, and thus to brighten the devil in the death of a Christian man. But we are all equal, lord King, your men and theirs, when they are here in this land. You should think of this, when you sit here in this world as chieftain and judge over the people, that you represent on earth the judge who in the Day of Judgement will judge all the world. Now you must judge rightly, lord, for much is at stake, and not wrongly, for to every Thing and meeting comes Almighty God himself with his holy men. God comes to look after good men and right judgments, but so also comes the devil to look after men of wicked work and wrong judgments, and without doubt, that Judge shall come at the last when all things shall be judged rightly. Consider now lord King, which fire would be hotter and longer, that which is lighted in the oak logs in the oven, or that which is lighted in dry sticks? Now if you, lord, make a wrong judgment, then you will be thrown into the fire which is lighted in the oak logs, but if you judge rightly, according to your understanding, then there is a likelihood that you will only cleanse yourself in cleansing flames made from the dry sticks."

Thus Jon the priest ended his speech.

The King said, "You have spoken harshly, priest." But he was not seen to be greatly angered towards him.

Then Gisl stood up and said, "Will you allow me, lord, to say a few words?"

The King asked who spoke now. It was told to him.

"I won't forbid it," said the King.

Gisl said, "I shall speak then and say that my father was slain by the hand of Gjafvald and Thormod. I was then six years old, and Thorvald, my brother, nine. We were present when my father was killed, and Gjafvald said we two brothers must both be slain. It is not manly to speak of this, lord, but at that time I began to cry."

The King said, "You have boldly removed the stigma of those cries."

Gisl said, "It is truly said, lord, that I have for a long time this spring waited to waylay Gjafvald. But then twice when it seemed to me the best chance for it, I respected the church--once in the church, and once as the None-ringing began. It was for my respecting the church that the None-ringing gave me life. But I've made a poem about you and I want to have a hearing."

The King said, "Recite it if you wish."

Gisl recited the poem boldly, but there wasn't much art in the poem.

Afterwards, Gisl said to Teit, "You have shown me great kindness, and now I want you not to run a risk any longer. I wish to go into the hands of King Magnus and offer him my head."

"Do as you wish," said Teit.

Gisl then dropped his weapons, went across the meeting room and laid his head on the King's knee. Then he said, "Do with my head whatever seems best. I will be thankful if you give me life and make me such a man as you think fit."

The King answered, "Keep your head, and go to Gjafvald's place at the table. There take food and drink and hold such attendance on me as he held before. I do this mostly for the wishes of Gjafvald, my friend. Now, eight Icelanders must come forward as surety. I judge sixteen marks of gold for the slaying of Gjafvald. Half of this fine shall be forgiven for the wrong committed against you, but the eight of your surety men must pay one mark each."

They thanked the King and agreed to this.

Then the King said to Jon the Priest, "Your pleading well-pleased me. You have spoken on God's behalf. I eagerly wish to be in your prayers, for they will have great sway with God. I believe that your will and the will of God go together."

He granted the King's request.

One day when Jon the priest walked down the street, a man said to him, "Go into that lodging. Sigurd Wool-Rope wants to meet with you."

He did so and Sigurd said, "There is no doubt, priest, that your words have bitten me, because I am sick. I would like you to sing prayers over me."

He did so and made the sign of the cross over him. Then Sigurd said, "Great are the powers of your words, both harsh and good, because now I feel better." Sigurd gave good gifts to Jon the priest, and they parted friends.

It was for this that Sigurd soon settled into the monk's life at Nidarholm, giving great gifts to the monastery there. After this Jon the priest and

Teit Bishopson went to Iceland. Jon the priest became the bishop at Holar and later was made a saint.

Notes on the Story of Gisl Illugason

[1]King Magnus Bareleg ruled Norway from 1093 to 1103.

[2]This seems to be an attempt to disguise himself as a leper.

[3]This is possibly some bravura on Gisl's part. The name Vigfus means "eager to slay" and Ofeig means "not fated to die."

[4]Jon, who figures largely in the rest of this story, became the Bishop of Northern Iceland in 1106. The saga about him, *Jóns saga helga*, written by the monk Gunnlaug Leifsson, contains many accounts of his miracles as well as a radically different version of this story of Gisl at Magnus' court.

[5]This term of abuse probably originated in the Icelanders' custom of supporting themselves primarily with cattle and sheep.

[6]The ringing of the bell at Nones (the office of the ninth hour, 3 p.m.) on the day before a holy day proclaimed the start of the holy day, and executions were prohibited during the course of the holy day.

THE SAGA OF BJORN, CHAMPION OF HITARDALE

Chapter 1--Thord, Bjorn, and Oddny

It must now be told of those Icelanders who lived in the days of King Olaf Haraldson and were close friends with the King. The first of these was the noble Thorkel Eyjolfson. He had married Gudrun, Osvif's daughter, and he was always well-honored by King Olaf whenever he journeyed to Norway.

Also in this time one Thord Kolbeinson lived at Hitarness in Iceland. He wa a great skald and very much valued his renown. Always was he highly honored abroad by powerful men for his skill and wit. Thord became one of Jarl Erik Hakonson's men and was much valued by him; yet, Thord was not much liked by the common folk because he mocked and insulted those who seemed to him easy to deal with.

A man called Bjorn grew up with Skuli Thorsteinson at Borg. He was the son of Arngeir and Thordis, daughter of Thorfin the Strong and Saeun, daughter of Skalla-Grim. Bjorn grew early to a great size, and he was manly, strong, and handsome. Along with many others, Bjorn had also been the butt of Thord's mocking and spite. For this reason he lived with his kinsman, Skuli, when he was young. He felt he was better off there than with his father due to the unfriendliness of Thord Kolbeinson. What went on between Bjorn and Thord before Bjorn went to Skuli's is not of great moment to this saga, and so will not be told. Skuli, though, was quite pleased with Bjorn and greatly honored him. His wisdom told him Bjorn would become a most valued man to have in the family. Bjorn was quite happy wth his lot while he stayed with Skuli.

At Hjorsey Island, out from Myra, lived Thorkel, the son of Dugfus the Rich from Dugfusdale. Thorkel was a wealthy man and a good householder. He had a daughter named Oddny, a beautiful woman and worthy of note. She was called Oddny Eykyndil[1] Bjorn used to go to Hjorsey Island, and when he did, he always stopped to talk to Oddny and soon they both began to like each other. It was said by many that if Bjorn were to marry her, it would be an equal match, for he was the most manly of men and well skilled.

Chapter 2--The Betrothal

When Bjorn had been with Skuli for five years, the news came that a ship had landed at Gufuaross. The ship was manned by Norwegians. The farmer Skuli rode at once to the ship and bid the traders stay with him, for it was his custom to get the friendship of traders by treating them well. After the ship was beached, three of the traders went to stay with him. Bjorn was eager to help and serve the traders, and they liked him well. It wasn't long before Bjorn went to speak with Skuli and ask if he could sail abroad with these men. Skuli took this well and said, which was true, that these men were quite successful and that many young men were less ready for such an undertaking than Bjorn. Skuli added that he would also help Bjorn with what was needed. Bjorn thanked him for this offer and for all the help Skuli had given him before, then he settled the matter with the ship's traders. From his father and Skuli Bjorn got a good deal of money for the trip, so he could go in honor with these noble men.

There is little more to say about the traders until the spring when they went down to the ship, got it ready, and waited for a fair wind. When this happened, Bjorn rode up to meet with Skuli. When they met, Bjorn said he wanted only one thing else before he left, and that was Oddny, Thorkel's daughter. Skuli asked whether he had said anything to her about this. Bjorn said he sure had!

"Then we shall go," said Skuli, and so they did. They went to Hjorsey Island and met with Thorkel and his daughter, Oddny. Bjorn began the talk by asking for Oddny's hand in marriage. Thorkel took this well, but he left it up to his daughter. Oddny agreed, for there had long been a great love between her and Bjorn.

They then pledged their troth. Oddny would stay betrothed for three years, but should Bjorn be kept from marrying her in the fourth year, then she must wait for him. However, if he just didn't come home from Norway within three years, then Thorkel could give her to someone else if he wished. Bjorn must also send men out to renew the betrothal if he himself was kept from coming. Skuli then laid out for Bjorn so much money that it not only covered the bride-price, for Oddny, but it just about equaled all that Thorkel owned.[2]

After this they parted, and Skuli came with Bjorn back to the ship.

He said, "When you get to Norway, Bjorn, find my friend, Jarl Erik. Take him my greetings and the message that I wish him to receive you. Take him also a token this gold piece, for then he will believe that this is indeed my wish."

Bjorn thanked Skuli for all the goodwill he had been shown since he first came to him, and they then parted. This all happened in the latter part of the days of Jarl Erik.

They sailed early in the summer. The journey was uneventful, and they made land in Norway. Bjorn quickly found Jarl Erik and gave him Skuli's greetings and the token. The Jarl took this well and said he would eagerly do what was asked. He added, "And you, Bjorn, shall indeed be welcome." Bjorn said he had surely hoped for that.

He then joined the Jarl's men where he was held in good esteem.

Chapter 3 -- Thord's Promise to Bjorn

Early that same summer a Norwegian ship landed in Iceland at Straumfjord. Thord Kolbeinson rode to this ship, and when he found out they meant to return to Norway, he made known his wish to go abroad and bought a share in the ship. Thord had a kinsman in Denmark called Hroi the Rich. He had a farm in Hroiskeld, and Thord was his sole heir. Thord then made ready for the voyage out, but he was somewhat late in getting away.

The Jarl's men heard that Thord was coming to Norway from Iceland in the same ship which had left earlier, and that he was now the ship's master and was bringing a poem to the Jarl. The Jarl asked Bjorn if he knew Thord. Bjorn said he knew Thord quite well and that he was a good skald, and he added, "That poem he made will be a good one."

The Jarl said, "Does it seem wise to you, Bjorn, for me to listen to the poem?"

"Indeed so," said Bjorn, "for it will bring honor to you both."

A little while later Thord came to meet the Jarl and greeted him politely. The Jarl took this well and asked who this man might be. He said he was an Icelander called Thord, and he added, "I wish that you would listen to the poem I've made about you." The Jarl said that would be fine. Thord recited the poem. It was a *drápa* and well-made. The Jarl was pleased with it and bid Thord stay with him the winter. Thord agreed, and was treated well by the Jarl. Both Thord and Bjorn stayed that winter with the Jarl.

Some of the Jarl's men told him that Bjorn and Thord were not friends, and one time the Jarl called Thord before him and asked if he knew Bjorn and if so, why would Skuli have sent this man to him. Thord answered that Bjorn was the bravest of men, and he added, "I know Bjorn well, and Skuli sent him to you because he hasn't another kinsman of greater worth."

"That may be true," said the Jarl.

Thord said, "Have you yet learned how old Bjorn is?"

"No," said the Jarl.

Thord said, "He is now eighteen years old, and though you have many bold men with you already, Bjorn will be seen to be among the bravest."

The Jarl was pleased with this, and Thord didn't let it be known that things hadn't always been so good between him and Bjorn.

One day in the winter Thord met Bjorn and bade him drink with him, and he added, "We've now come to a point where things can't go on being bad between us. That one quarrel we had is of little worth, and so let things be well between us from now on." Bjorn agreed, and things went on in this way until Yule.

On the eighth day of Yule Jarl Erik gave his men gifts, in the custom of chieftains of other lands.[4] For Bjorn's bravery and because he was Skuli's kinsman, the Jarl gave him a gold ring that weighed half a mark. He gave Thord a costly sword as a reward for his poem.

One evening that winter Thord spoke to Bjorn. They were both drunk, though Bjorn was more so. Thord said, "What are your plans, come spring? Are you going back to Iceland?"

"I'm not going to Iceland in the summer," said Bjorn, "because I'm going to ask Jarl Erik's leave to go raiding. I would win goods and honor, if I can."

Thord answered, "That seems unwise to me. You already have honor and esteem. Why risk yourself in this? Why don't you go back to Iceland with me, and see to your marriage?"

Bjorn answered, "I'll not go back this summer."

Thord said, "Your plan seems unwise to me, to leave a land where you already have a lot of riches and not know whether you'll come back or not."

"Nothing risked, nothing gained," said Bjorn, "so I'm going raiding."

Thord said, "Then send Oddny, your betrothed, the ring the Jarl gave you. Entrust it to me. This will show her you still love her and are earnest about her if you send her such a costly gift. Also, you'll be in her thoughts more often, and not likely to be forgotten. On the other hand, if you go back to Iceland, as we hope you will, then you get both the ring and the woman and all the money that was promised along with her. And it is also true that there's no better match in Iceland than Oddny."

Bjorn said, "You speak truly, Thord, that Oddny is the most honorable of women and fully a match for me in all ways, and had you treated me in Iceland as you do now, I would do all that you ask. But now I think I would be mistaken to trust you, and it would be said that I had little regard for the Jarl's gift if I yielded the ring to your keeping."

Thord told him to hold to his marriage promises. Bjorn said he had men to renew the betrothal, if needed, and he added, "And you, Thord, tell the truth about why I'm doing this when you get to Iceland. My courage has been little tested, and I still have little of the battle skills of better men. If I went to Iceland now, I couldn't easily leave my marriage."

Thord promised he would, and added, "Then I ask you for the ring, to give weight to my words. Bjorn, there's no need to fear I'll betray you. I will be true."

"I'll risk it," said Bjorn, "this one time, but if you are false to me, I'll never trust you again." Bjorn then put the Jarl's gift ring into Thord's hand and bade him take it to Oddny. Thord promised to do so. He then talked very agreeably with Bjorn, making many avowals of doing his task well and of faithfulness. After this they parted, for the time being. Later, when he was sober, Bjorn thought he had said too much to Thord and had trusted him too far.

The winter passed, and Thord got his ship ready. He met Bjorn and they talked once more of this.

"Remember what we've said, Thord," said Bjorn, "and fare well with my errand."

Thord promised he would surely do so, and they parted on pretty good terms. Men couldn't quite figure out this turn of events with Bjorn and Thord, but they knew Thord was fifteen years older than Bjorn. The _drápa_ Thord had made about Jarl Erik was called _Belgskaka-drápa_.

Thord put to sea early in the summer and landed in Iceland during the Althing in Gufuaross. He rode at once to the Thing and men crowded around him because he knew how to tell the news so well. He carried out Bjorn's errand, then, and said Bjorn would come to look after the marriage, and he gave Oddny the ring. But he added that Bjorn had given him the marriage, if he died or failed to return to Iceland.

Chapter 4--Bjorn Becomes a Champion

That same summer Thord went to Iceland, Bjorn went before the Jarl and asked his leave to go raiding in the east. The Jarl bade him go if he wished. So Bjorn went east into Russia, to meet King Valdimar,[5] and he stayed there during the winter, treated well by the King. He was well-liked by the King's nobles, for his bearing and temper.

It is said that Bjorn was in Russia with King Valdimar when an all powerful army came to the land. It was by the champion called Kaldimar, a large man of great strength. He was a close kinsman of the King, the greatest of fighters, skilled at arms, and the bravest of men. It was said that King Valdimar and the champion had equal claim to the kingdom, but the champion had not gotten the kingdom because he was younger. For this reason he had gone into raiding to seek renown for himself, and now no one, in all the eastern lands, equaled his fame.[6]

When King Valdimar heard of his coming, he sent men to his kinsman with peace terms. He bid him come in peace and take over half the kingdom. But the champion said he must rule the kingdom alone. He said if the King didn't want that, then they could either settle the matter by single combat or with their armies. Neither plan seemed good to Valdimar. He very much didn't want to lose his men, and he himself had never been trained in single combat. He asked his men for advice. They told him to get more troops and fight. In a short time they got together there a great host of men, and King Valdimar went up against the champion. However, before battle the King offered to let a man fight in single combat in his place. The champion agreed to this on these terms--that he would get all the kingdom if he slew that man, but that if he fell, then the King would own the kingsom as before. Then the King searched among his men for one who would fight for him, but the men were not eager for this. It seemed to them sure death to fight the champion. The King then promised his close friendship and other honors if someone would risk it, but no one would.

Then Bjorn said, "A man who won't help his lord in need I see only as craven. I left my land to seek fame, and there are now only two choices at hand--through valor to get victory, though that is unlikely against this foe, or to fall proudly, sword in hand. Surely is that better than a life of shame for not daring to win honor for one's King. I shall fight Kaldimar!"

The King thanked Bjorn. The laws for single combat were then spoken. The champion had a sword, called Maering, which was the greatest of treasures. Bjorn and the champion fought both hard and quickly, and it ended with the champion falling to his death before Bjorn, though Bjorn himself was gravely wounded.

For this Bjorn got much honor from the King, and his renown spread widely. The King had a tent pitched over Bjorn, because it seemed to him Bjorn could not be carried away. The King himself then went home. Bjorn and his men stayed in the tent, and when his wounds had begun to heal, Bjorn made this verse:

(1) Now would Lofn's fair hand*
Eykyndil, sleep as my lover--
And soar would my song--
If it were known
By the fair linen-stay (woman)

That though now in a tent
With four spear-bearers
I have won great fame.[7]

*woman--Lofn is an Eddaic love goddess

Later on, Bjorn was carried to the King's home with great honor. The King gave him all of the champion's bettle gear and the sword Maering. For his deeds men called Bjorn a champion, and he was still called this even many years later in his own district in Iceland.

Bjorn lay wounded during the summer, and the following winter he stayed in Russia. By then he had been abroad three years. At this point he left for Norway, but by the time he got there it was late in the summer and all the ships had gone to Iceland.

Chapter 5--Oddny's Marriage

The summer before, Thord learned from some traders in Hvita that Bjorn had been wounded. He made a deal with them to spread the word that Bjorn had died, and so they did. Later, Thord began to talk openly of Bjorn's death. He said men had told him when he had been buried. No one was able to gainsay this, and it was thought unlikely that Thord would lie. Later on, Thord came to Hjorsey Island and asked for Oddny's hand in marriage. Her kinsmen didn't want to give her to him before the time that they and Bjorn had agreed on had passed. They said they would talk over the matter in the summer, if they still heard nothing of Bjorn after the ships had come.

Soon the ships came from Norway, but the men on them knew nothing of Bjorn, for he had not reached Norway before they put to sea. So Thord pressed his case, and Oddny was given to him.

While Bjorn and his men were making ready to sail, a ship sailed into the harbor from the sea. The ship had come from Iceland, so Bjorn and his men took a boat and rowed out to it to get the news.

They were told of Oddny's marriage. When Bjorn heard that he said he did not wish to go to Iceland.

That winter Bjorn stayed with Jarl Erik and his men, and when they sailed to Hamarsey island, Bjorn made this verse:

(2) The hand of fire of Hrist*
Was made by a man
To joy in the flesh-bone's delight.
The thrust-muscle pins Eykyndil
Hard on the down bed,
While stiff oars we bend.
Someone's behind all this--
But I'm bid to row this ship.

*woman--hand fire = gold of Hrist (a valkyrie) = woman

Bjorn was still held in the same high esteem as before by the Jarl.

The next summer Bjorn journeyed west to England. He was well-received there and stayed two years with Canute the Great. Once it so happened when Bjorn sailed with the King and his men in the south that a flying dragon flew over the ship and attacked the King's men. The dragon swooped down on a man, but Bjorn was standing beside him and threw his shield over him. The dragon nearly tore through the shield. Bjorn then grabbed the dragon's tail with one hand and with his sword struck the beast just behind the wings. At this, the dragon split apart and fell down dead. For this the King gave Bjorn much money and a good longship.

With this ship Bjorn soon sailed to Denmark where he went into a partnership with Audun Back-Flap, a Norwegian from Vik, but who had some kinsmen in Denmark. Audun had been outlawed from Norway. Bjorn held two ships in partnership with Audun and they would sail east and raid along the coast of Sweden during the summer, while spending the winters in Denmark. They did this for three years.

Chapter 6--Bjorn Goes Raiding

For some time Thord stayed at home in Hitarness, and men thought that Oddny was now even a better match than before, for her money, her family, and other honors. Thord and Oddny seemed to be getting on well. They had eight children, five sons and three daughters. Thord had by now sold that ship to traders which he had used in his travels.

All this time Bjorn was raiding to earn money and honor. He was still a friend of Jarl Erik, and the same men as before were still with him. He little longed for Iceland when he heard the news from there how Thord had plotted against him. Also in this time while Bjorn was away from Iceland there was a change of rulers in Norway. From Jarl Erik the kingdom went to Jarl Hakon, his son, but Svein, Erik's brother, still ruled his part of the land as before, and things stood this way for two years.

At that point Olaf the Holy came to the land and seized Hakon in Saudungsund. Hakon swore oaths to King Olaf and later left the land. Olaf then fought with Jarl Svein at Nesjar on Palm Sunday and made Svein flee. After this, Olaf became King over all the land. The news that Jarl Erik and Jarl Hakon had left the land soon spread to other lands, and it wasn't long before Bjorn and his men heard about this change in rulers. They heard many good rumors about this worthy King.

Also about this time there was a man of note called Thorkel Eyjolfson out on a trading voyage. He was held in great honor by King Olaf. Thorkel was also a friend of Thord Kolbeinson.

Chapter 7--Bjorn and Thord Meet Again

Later it was said that Thord Kolbeinson learned of the death of Hroi the Rich, his mother's brother. Thord was his heir, and he then bought a ship, meaning to go abroad to fetch Hroi's goods. He journeyed first to Norway to seek out King Olaf, and he was welcomed there. He told the King why he had come. Thorkel was there also and pleaded Thord's case well with the King, that he should get what belonged to him. The King had a letter written to a friend of his in Denmark and placed his seal on it. With Thord at this time were the sons of Eid, Thorkel and Thorgrim, and also Kalf the Spiteful.

Thord had made a *drápa* about King Olaf. He went before the King and recited it himself. For this he got from the King a gold ring, a silk coat trimmed with lace, and a good sword. Quietly, Thord asked if men had heard anything about Bjorn. He was told that Bjorn had gone off raiding with many men.

Thord had a small ship, but he had a number of men from Vik aboard. In all, there were nearly thirty in the ship. That summer he sailed to Denmark into Hroiskeld and got quite a bit from the estate, though much had already been taken. Towards the end of the summer they went north, laying a course for Brenney islands.[8] There were many islands there and they were sparsely settled. Often were these islands raided by vikings, for there were many hidden coves there, and the land was covered with forests.

Bjorn was sailing among these coves, and it was already late in the day when he saw two tongues of land that jutted out from the main island. One was called Thraelaeyr and the other Oddaeyr. There Bjorn anchored his ship. That same evening Thord got to the island and anchored this ship there for the night.

Later, two men came up to the ship from the forest and asked who owned the ship. A quick-tongued man recklessly said Thord Kolbeinson owned it.

"Your tongue is rash," said Thord, "tell them Thorar the Far-Traveler owns the ship."

He did so, and the man from the forest said, "Do as you wish; lie or tell the truth." The men then turned back. They were Bjorn's scouts. He was anchored on the other side of the island with nine ships.

When the men had left, Thord said, "They will have been somebody's scouts, and I'm going ashore now to see what I can find out."

When his men came back and told him about Thord, Bjorn said to Audun, "From what they say, I think it must be Thord's ship. It's only fitting that we should find it."

When Thord got back to the ship, he said to those who had gone out with him that he thought Bjorn wouldn't be far away, and he added, "Now I want you to say that I'm still back in Denmark and haven't yet got the money, in case it happens, as I think it will, that Bjorn isn't far away and means to come here. In the meantime, I'll hide."

Kalf the Spiteful said, "That would be a good plan if you aren't found, otherwise, however, great shame will come to you. I would rather defend our goods and lives as long as we can."

"My plan is better," said Thord, "all of you will be left alone. He wants only me."

Thord then went ashore and hid behind a bush under the bank and watched the ship. He covered himself with a cloak.

Soon Bjorn told his men to arm themselves and head for the trading ship. He believed the first thing said was the truth, that Thord Kolbeinson was the ship's master. They did as Bjorn said and went up to the ship. It seemed to them the ship was without a leader. Bjorn then asked who the master of the ship was. The men on Thord's ship weren't very happy to see Bjorn, but they went along with Thord's story. Bjorn didn't believe it and wanted to search the island.

They first ransacked the ship, but didn't find him, so they began to search the island. There were nearly two hundred men looking. When Bjorn and his men got to where Thord was hiding, Thord sprang up and welcomed Bjorn.

"So you are here, Thord," said Bjorn, "and not in Demnark. Why are you shaking? Tell us the news from Iceland. It has been long since we last met."

"I can tell of many things," said Thord.

"Where were you in the winter," said Bjorn.

"With the King in Norway," answered Thord.

Bjorn said, "Where in the land was the King?"

"He was in the north," said Thord, "and when spring came, he went east to Vik, and he's there now."

Bjorn said, "What's the latest news from Iceland?"

The death of Skuli," said Thord, "but your father and foster-father still live."[9]

Bjorn said, "Skuli's death is indeed big news, but tell me, is it true that you married Oddny, Thorkel's daughter, shortly after we parted?"

Thord said it was true.

Bjorn said, "Did that seem to you a faithful way to keep our friendship?"

Thord said, "I didn't know she should wait for you longer than three years."

Bjorn said, "Such a quibble won't help you. I've long known the whole truth about this."

Thord asked to atone for it.

"It's a better idea," said Bjorn, "that you be slain, and thus end the matter between us."

It ended this way. Bjorn spared his life, but he took Thord's money and the trading ship. Then he stripped Thord of all his treasures and left him in a most wretched way. Thord asked to keep his goods, but he wasn't allowed to, and Bjorn made Thord and his men get into the ship's boat with only their clothes, and told them to sail in this way to the mainland. Before they parted, Bjorn said, "Thord, now you've lost your money and been shamed and dishonored, but it is still less than you deserve. Go now to the Orkney islands, but spend little time in Norway. I shall go to meet the King. I honor him so greatly without even having seen him that I won't slay you while you're his guest, but should I ever meet you henceforth, no safety will you find, anywhere."

Thord and his men then went to the boat. With them went the men from Vik. They wanted to keep their belongings, but they only got to keep their weapons. Later on they met with the King and told him about the unlawful taking of goods and about Bjorn's accusing of Thord.

Chapter 8--King Olaf's Settlement

After this Bjorn met with his partner, Audun, and said he wanted to see King Olaf, and he added, "I don't want his anger to fall on me for the taking of the traders' goods." Audun said he would follow him since he was homesick and wanted to return to Norway.

They went to meet the King, but left behind most of their men with the money and the ship. Three nights later they found the King. Thord and his men were there. Bjorn and his men, twelve together, went into the hall where the King sat drinking. Fifty men had been left behind in the ship. Bjorn went before the King and greeted him with honor. The King asked who he might be. Bjorn told his name.

The King said, "Is this not your enemy, Thord?"

Thord said he sure was. The King said he was a bold man to dare to come here, and he bid his men seize Bjorn and put him in irons. Bjorn said that was easy enough to do, but he added that he thought himself hardly without grounds against Thord. the King said his vikings, in their greed, had found it all too easy to rob the traders. Bjorn spoke up then and told about his dealings with Thord Kolbeinson from the beginning and what he accused Thord of. the King asked Thord if what Bjorn said was true. Thord said he had what he thought were true reports of Bjorn's death.

"You have not proved that," said the King, "and it seems to me Bjorn has a good case against you. Do you want me now to judge the matter?"

Both Thord and Bjorn agreed to this and to keep peace with each other. In the King's judgement the woman and all her money and goods were to go to Thord, but to Bjorn went an equal amount to what Oddny had received as heir to her father. The dishonor of both deeds, the money taking and the woman taking, was to be equal. Bjorn was to get a fine coat and a ring for the ring which Thord got with Oddny. Thord was to keep that sword which the King had given him. The King said things would fare better with them if they kept this settlement well. Bjorn got all the goods Thord had there with him, except the ship, but had to return to each trader the money he had taken from him.

Thord, Kalf, and the sons of Eid all stayed the winter with the King, but Bjorn went east to Vik with Audun and his men, for whom Bjorn had gotten the King's safe conduct. They stayed there for the winter. In the summer he went back to King Olaf and stayed with him two years. Thord went back to Iceland in the summer but said nothing about what happened with Bjorn in the east. King Olaf had given Thord a shipment of wood before he left.

Chapter 9--Bjorn's Friendship with King Olaf

Bjorn stayed with the King, and one time while the King and Bjorn were chatting, Bjorn said, "I know, lord, that I've been slandered by some in this matter between Thord and me. But were you also told what it was that kept me from killing Thord and his men?"

The King said, "I was not told of that."

Bjorn said, "then I shall tell you. Even though I had never seen you, I held you in such esteem that I didn't slay Thord and his ship's crew because he had been your winter guest. I would kill him should we meet again, but only if you were out of the matter, so it wouldn't offend you."

The King said, "We shall now send for those men who told us, and they will say the truth, for we've found them to be good men."[10]

This was done, and the men avowed that Bjorn had, in fact, said it was out of respect for the King that he didn't kill Thord and his crew. The King now thought Bjorn the worthier, for giving up Thord for his sake. There were also men with the King who knew of all the dealings between Bjorn and Thord and who had been with Jarl Erik, and all this was told to the King. Thus Bjorn's story was backed by many.

The King said, "It is now also right that Thord's crew got their money in my judgement, but Thord got only peace with you."[11]

Bjorn said he wouldn't have spared Thord except out of regard for the King.

"You shall be a greater friend to me now than before," said the King, but he told Bjorn also that there was only honor in keeping the agreement he had made between them.

"I wish also," said the King, "that you would stop raiding. Though it may seem to suit you well, it happens often to disturb God's law."

Bjorn said it would be so and that he was happy to stay with the King.

The King said, "You are much to my liking, but it is not fated for us to be together for a long time, because my friend Thorkel Eyjolfson is due to come here, and he would quickly take up Thord's quarrel with you. It is better that you go out to Iceland."

So it came to pass that Bjorn joined the King on his round of feasts that autumn. Their friendship remained fast and Bjorn received good gifts from him. It was customary at these feasts to provide every courtesy to the King, and at one of these feasts to which Bjorn went with the King, a large tub bath had been made, for no hot-springs were to be found in Norway. A tent was pitched over the bath, and after laying their clothes down in the field, the King and his men went into it. It was usual at this time for men to wear thongs. These were like a belt wrapped around the leg from the shoes to the knee. The noble men of the land almost always wore them, and so did the King and Bjorn. Bjorn left the bath to get dressed before the other men, and his clothes lay beside the King's. Bjorn didn't notice, until he got dressed, that he had put on the King's thongs by mistake, but when he did, he told the King at once of his carelessness. The King, however, hushed him and said Bjorn's thongs were no worse than his own. For the rest of his life Bjorn wore these thongs on his legs, and with them he was buried. Much later when his bones were dug up and moved to another church, these same thongs were found to be whole while all else had rotted. They are now serving as belts for the Mass vestments at Gard in Akraness.

Bjorn spent the next winter in Norway, and King Olaf gave him a costly cloak and pledged his friendship. he said Bjorn was a brave fighter and a good man.

Chapter 10--Bjorn Returns to Iceland

It is said that when spring came Bjorn got his ship ready for Iceland. At this time also another ship was making ready for Iceland and it left before Bjorn's ship. King Olaf sent word with these men that Thord should keep the settlement even if Bjorn should come to Iceland. He said Thord was all the more bound to it now.

In the summer Bjorn came out to Bordeyri in Hrutafjord. He arrived with a lot of money and much fame and renown. He and his men unloaded their goods from the ship and raised up a tent.

It is said that also that same evening Oddny began a talk with her husband, Thord.

"Have you heard any news, Thord?" she said.

"None," he said, but it looks as though you know something."

"Quite so," she said, "I have heard something which seems to be news to me. I heard that a ship came into Hrutafjord, and Bjorn is on it--Bjorn, who you said had died!"

"Do you find that noteworthy?" said Thord.

"It is surely news," she said, "and even more fully do I know now to whom I am married. I thought you to be a good man, but you are all lies and deceit."

"It is said that redress has been made for all," said Thord.

"I bet," said Oddny, "that he has gotten his own redress."

"Believe what you want," said Thord.

That was the end of their talk. Later Arngeir and Ingjald and their men went to the ship and met Bjorn.[12] The meeting was joyful, and they bid Bjorn stay with them. They said they were happy to see him, for they had been apart a long time.

Bjorn said he should go to his father's and later, when summer had passed and the ship been put up, Bjorn did go home to his father's.

Many were pleased with Bjorn's homecoming. Before this men had just about given up thinking about his fate, whether he were alive or not. Some said it was false that he was dead, and some said it was true. It was now clear what the truth was.

Bjorn was welcomed when he came home. His foster father gave him the hound, V---,[13] the one Bjorn had so admired before. His father gave him a horse called Hviting. It was all white in color and it came with two white foals. Those were good gifts.

Chapter 11--Thord's Invitation

It is said that Thord soon asked Oddny if she thought it wise to ask Bjorn to stay with them. He said he didn't want men to meddle and stir up trouble by gossiping, and he added, "By this I hope to prove to all he holds for me no ill will."

Oddny held back, saying that to judge from the talk then going around, this would be unwise. Thord wouldn't let his mind be changed, though, and he started for Holm in Hitardale. He rode alone and he wore a blue cape.

A mountain stood at the back of the house in Holm and a ridge ran down from the mountain to the house. Bjorn and his mother were at work that day. They were spreading out wet linen to dry. Suddenly she said, "A man is riding up. He wears a blue cape and looks very much like Thored Kolbeinson. It is Thord, and this surely means trouble."

"No it won't," said Bjorn. Thord came up. They greeted each other and asked the news. At last Thord said, "My errand here is to find out whether you will keep the settlement the King made between us, that neither of us henceforth need seek redress from the other. It is of note that a trustworthy man made this settlement between us. Still, I myself had some doubts for a while that we should settle."

Bjorn said keeping the settlement was the only thing to be done.

Thord said, "I've come away with the better part of the settlement, and I'll now show you that I, too, want to keep the agreement. I bid you to stay the winter at my home. I will keep you well, and I hope you'll take my offer."

So spoke Thord with winning words.

Thordis said, "I'll not be easily swayed by this. Think about this, Bjorn. The more smoothly he talks, the more falsely he thinks. Trust him not."

At this, Arngeir came up and asked what they were talking about. Thord told him.

"It seems to me," said Arngeir, "that going along with this will more likely result in greater friendship, if in fact, they have settled their differences. So I urge Bjorn to go, and Thord to make good his offer."

Arngeir stood at odds with his wife on this.

Bjorn said, "I think I will stay with my father. Gossip would find this invitation too strange." Thord spoke then and said that Bjorn would not be keeping faith with him if he didn't take up the offer. At last Bjorn promised that he would stay with him a while, but he said he must first spend some time with his father. Thord rode home and told Oddny where he'd been during the day, and he said he had now done what he wanted to.

Thord said he had bid Bjorn stay with then and he added he had made redress for getting her.

"I think," she said , "you lie when you say that."

Thord said, "A single oath doesn't break all the others."[14]

So they ended their talk.

Chapter 12--Bjorn and Thord Exchange Some Verses

Bjorn made ready to stay with Thord. He left for Hitarness with three things of great value, two horses and a hound. He rode one horse and kept the other in tow. His money and his goods he left back in Holm. Thord welcomed him. He seated Bjorn at table nearest himself and bade his men treat him well. The men promised to do this, though most thought it strange that Bjorn should be staying there. Some time passed, and things seemed to be going well.

But it is said that at one time in the beginning of winter Thord came to ask Oddny how the farm work was going.

"Many people are around here now," he added, "and everybody must have something to do."

In the Hitara river lies an island with meadows and grain fields, well-stocked with wild bird eggs and seals.

"Now men and women must go to the island to gather corn," Thord said, "but you must stay at home to milk the sheep that are rounded up during the day, though you are unused to this kind of work."

Oddny said, "Well, I'm looking at a fitting man to shovel out the sheep pen. You try that!"

"Wrong you are," said Thord, "for I've always done more work on this farmstead than you!" He was greatly upset by this and he struck Oddny's cheek with his right hand. Bjorn wasn't far away when this happened and he heard what went on. He made this verse:

(3) The wise lady bids a dainty boy
To shovel out the sheep pen.
The Rhine embers bearer*
Is not unjust in this.
The noble Hlokk of Rokkva's fire,+
The one called Eykyndil,
Bids me quickly hasten
Out from my door.

*woman--Rhine embers = gold; gold bearer = woman
+woman--Rokkva's (sea god) fire = gold; Hlokk (valkyrie) of gold = woman

Thord went on to work, but Oddny didn't milk the sheep and Thord didn't shovel out the pen. Thord didn't like Bjorn's poem, but he was quiet about it for a while.

Sometime later it is said that when Thord came home one day he saw Bjorn talking with the women. It was in the evening, and Bjorn was quite merry with them. Thord said this:

(4) Out shall you go!
Your girl flirting
Seems ill to me.
There you sit
In the evenings
When home we come,
As gay as I'd be.
Out shall you go!

Bjorn said, "So you still like to make poems like you used to in the old days," and he answered it with this verse:

(5) Here I shall sit!
And loudly sing
With skill to amuse
Your woman.
Should no blame
Fall on her or me.
Pure is my mind,
Here I shall sit!

A little later in the evening Thord came into the house very quietly. He wanted to know what was being said. He heard some voices which he thought were Bjorn and Oddny. He tried to overhear what they said. But Bjorn was aware of this and told Oddny that Thord was listening to them. Oddny took this very poorly, got very mad and left. Bjorn made this verse:

(6) Eykyndil, praised by all,
Sobbing now, would tell me something.
The love-searching woman
Best amuses me with her talk.
But a little boy would eavesdrop
On the drinking horn of Jord;*
Secretly he hid himself
And eagerly he listened.

*woman--Jord is an Eddaic goddess

Thord was not at all pleased with Bjorn's verse making, and although he said nothing for now, he clearly thought about it a lot. One evening in the hall Thord put Oddny on his knee and flirted with her. He wanted to know how Bjorn would take it. He kissed her and then made this verse:

(7) Bjorn should remember
The proud Jord of rings (woman)
Slipped from his grasp.
Fated for me it was
The head-band's holder to have (woman)
The rogue won't enjoy
The slender woman.
Such is for the better.

"So it happened," said Bjorn, "that I had to allow this marriage, but there are some things between us that will be slowly forgotten." Bjorn then made this verse:

(8) Should you also remember,
Thord,when your men we spared,
There at Thraelaeyr.
Little honor had you
When you left there,
Greatly bereft of goods.
Though you talked full well,
'Twas oft the lighter load you carried.

And he followed it quickly with this verse:

(9) You may remember, little boy,
When fear with fury
Shook your proud head.
I bid no one be hurt;
Yet fearful away you fled,
From the horse of the wind, (ship)
As fast as your feet would go,
With naught in mind but fear.

Still it seemed to Bjorn he hadn't stuck Thord hard enough for boasting about getting Oddny while Bjorn couldn't do anything about it, so he made this verse:

(10) Since you went and married
This thorn land holder,*
This, I'll tell in revenge
Your honor, Thord, lessens,
Coward that you are.
In Brenney Islands you hid
At Oddaeyr on the bank,
Just so we wouldn't meet!

*woman--land of thorns = jewelry; jewelry holder = woman

Now for a while it was quiet, but each one thought worse of the other than before, and soon Bjorn made this verse:

(10) You weren't exactly happy,
Weakling, when in Solundir
Money and goods were taken--
Many's the battle I fought--
There I, for valor known,
Ships and goods took away,
For your tricks, boaster.
For you, wretch, a just reward.[15]

It was no surprise that Thord didn't like the verse, and he became cold and surly with everyone. It is said that one evening Bjorn sat beside Oddny and insulted Thord yet again when he made this verse:

(12) Shall the wearer of thin cloth
Who west by the mountains lives
Prove a guess of her man--
The hand of Rind woke me first to love*
If she, the proud woman
With the wielder of the sun's sea+
Had a son who looks like me
This I'd like to know.[16]

*woman--Rind is a goddess
+man, Thord--sea's sun = gold; gold wielder = man

After this the verse making stopped, and they had no more to do with each other.

Chapter 13--Bjorn's Hound and his Horse

One evening later on, Thord came to speak with Oddny. He said, "You and many others tell me Bjorn is a fair man, but he doesn't seem so to me in some ways. He puts his hound under the table where it eats as much as any one of us. I've done nothing about this up till now, but I'll bet he'll get tired of this business if the food is cut down."

Oddny said, "Are you going to press this thing to an end?"

"Indeed I am," said Thord, "each man shall now get only buttered bread, and we shall see then whether the hound gets any of that. And another thing, Bjorn brought two horses here for the winter, and he tricks my houseman into feeding them. It's a mean trick to get them to feed the horses."

Later on, when the food had been cut, Bjorn gave the hound no less than before, even though there was less to eat. The servants, however, threatened to leave due to the cut in food. Before long Thord told Oddny he was no longer of a mind to starve for Bjorn's hound, and this was getting nowhere. The full ration had to come back. This was done, and it pleased the servants well. Bjorn, however, made as though he didn't notice the change. Thord often told Oddny Bjorn seemed to him largely ungrateful, and quite unbending in all this. Thord made a verse:

(13) Of happy mind, Hlin's gold,*
Were our house's silver,
At peace they lived
Together in our home.
Until the proud foe
Of landholder's light+
Among us awakened
The wailing of wolves.

*woman--Hlin = Odin's wife
+man, Bjorn--land-holder = sea; light of sea = gold; foe of gold = man

During the rest of the winter there was little peace between Bjorn and Thord, much to Oddny's distress. At first, Thord had promised Bjorn that his horses would either be pastured in Hitarness or fed in the home meadow. Bjorn had wanted them to be pastured out, but time passed and it wasn't done. One time, Kalf the Spiteful came to Hitarness. He asked Thord how he liked his winter guest, and whether he thought it wise that the greater part of the home meadow was eaten by Bjorn's horses, rather than his own. After a while they went to see the hay, and they thought it was in bad shape. Thord didn't like this at all and he told Oddny Bjorn must have tricked his houseman to trample the hay in the dirt and spoil it. Oddny said Bjorn would have had no part in that and that his horses were fed apart from the others. She added, "And you, Thord, should mind that you fulfill all you promised him."

After this, Thord had Bjorn's horses driven out into Hitarness, where they had good pasturage. Thord stopped grumbling about Bjorn's horses, and things were more or less quiet for a time.

Chapter 14--More Verses

Sometime later, it is said, Thord and Bjorn were quarreling with each other over drink one evening and Thord spoke this verse to Bjorn:

(14) Out shall you go!
Bad flour you sold
To me and said
That it was rye.
But when with water
It was mixed,
It was only ash.
Out shall you go!

Bjorn spoke this in reply:

(15) I shall sit quiet.
In autumn I came
And dearly bought
Old rotten lard.
You gave to me
A fair cloak
Quite full of holes.
I shall sit quiet.

It seemed that Thord felt his outlay for Bjorn was great, but no good came in return. Bjorn, however, paid him back in such a way because he felt Thord's invitation was really not heart-felt, since as a guest he was treated so shabbily. So he thought it only just to pay him back in kind. For both, now, matters were worse than before.

Thord, Oddny, and a work-woman who did their washing all slept in an outbuilding during the winter. One evening Oddny came to bed late, but Thord would give her no room in the bed. She climbed over the bedboard and tried to get under the covers beside him, but this was not possible, and she had to stay sitting up. About this Bjorn made a verse:

(16) The Ull of War-Gefn's spear,
Who hides his ugly habits,
So spreads across the bed
of Lodda's bed-dragon.
Njor of the dunes'ship*
Shivering lies in small space.
There's naught to praise in this,
The plight of a gentle Thrud's jewel.+

*woman--dunes' ship = sea; Njor of the sea = woman
+woman--Thrud is a valkyrie

Oddny then bade them not to compose about her and said this poem should not be spread around.

The winter passed and the summer came without Thord and Bjorn speaking further to each other. In the winter Oddny had said to Bjorn that he should take one of her daughters since he hadn't gotten her as had been planned in the first place, and one evening Bjorn remembered this and set the maids on his knee while he made this verse:

(17) Two sisters and their mother's love
Are by a bad skald loved and honored.
Well do I trust her words,
Yet they're still less than she.
So shall I for a while
Praise the field's necklace. (woman)
For a sea-fire giver*
There's no harm in that.

*man--sea fire = gold; gold giver = man

When summer came Bjorn got ready to leave. It is said that as he left the farm he gave Oddny the cloak Thord had given him, and they both wished each other well. Bjorn then rode to the out-building where Thord was. Kalf the Spiteful had just come to the farm and was staying there with Thord. Bjorn told Thord he was ready for his journey and meant to go now. Thord said that was fine with him, though it would have been better if it were sooner. Bjorn said he had known for a long time . . .[17]

Chapter 15--Thord and the Seal

One time, it is said, Thord Kolbeinson was down looking over his beach, and there he came upon a seal in an ice hole. It was ebbtide, and the ice surrounded the seal so it couldn't escape. Thord figured that if he went home for his weapons the tide would come in before he got back and he wouldn't get the seal. He didn't want that, so he tried to kill the seal right then. He did this, but not without mishap. The seal bit his thigh and wounded him. Thord went home and had the seal butchered. He meant to hide the bite, but he couldn't do this for long because the wound worsened and he had to take to his bed.

Bjorn was not [far from] his farm in Voll, and this news soon reached him.[18] Men were not short of words in talking of Thord's wounds, and Bjorn made this verse:

(18) Sick at home the gold-keeper (man)
Lies, while here good men learn
The pale white suet glutton
Wounded was with seal scratches.
But once over the sea-rocks
Waves began to fall, hopped
The wretch away over the rocks
Like a skipping stone!

Thord learned of this and had the poem told to him. He thought it very bad indeed, and just like Bjorn to do this. Thord didn't answer it at first, but stayed quiet.

Chapter 16--Bjorn and the Calf

Later on, it is said that one evening Thorgeir, one of Bjorn's housemen, spoke with Bjorn. He said he didn't think there was enough hay for the cattle he watched over and he asked Bjorn to go look at the fodder and see whether he thought it would last. Bjorn did as he was asked. They went to the cattle barn and Thorgeir went in first because he knew the way. A cow had just had a calf, which lay on the floor, however, and Thorgeir tripped and fell over it. He cursed at this, but Bjorn bade him throw the calf back up into the stall. Thorgeir said he thought it better this devil lay on the ground and he didn't want to move it. Bjorn then picked up the calf and thrust it back into the stall.

When they went home, Thorgeir told this to his friends. He said Bjorn picked a calf up off the floor and put it back in the stall, and he added, "But I wouldn't do it." There were guests at the farm, and they heard this tale of Thorgeir's. Not much later some men came to Hitarness and told it to Thord. Thord said Bjorn had enough men and women to see to such matters and that there was no need for him to attend to a cow's calving, and he made this verse:

(19) Tyrant, why should you
Sitting, dung-covered, at home
Be always praising my scratches,
As if the seal had wounded me.
To you it should be a sorrow,
O man of the shaking shield (coward)
That under its tail you grabbed
The backside of a calf.

Men felt it wise that this poem not be spread about, but it got out anyway and Bjorn heard it. He didn't like it at all and he didn't want to leave matters as they stood.

During the summer Bjorn rode to Hitarness with sixty men and summoned Thord for this poem which he felt had broken the law. Friends of both, however, said this case should not go before the Thing, that they should rather settle in the district. But that was not possible. Thord would not settle outside the

Thing. So, they settled before the Thing, and Thord had to pay a hundred silvers for the poem.[19] Bjorn also asked this in the law court, that either of them who spoke a verse with the hearing of the other should be outlawed. Those who sat in judgement agreed to this. It seemed better they both do less spattering of themselves with foul words. With this settlement they went home, and for the time being, it was more or less quiet.

Chapter 17--The Insult Pole

It is said that a while later something was found at Thord's harbor marker that didn't exactly seem very friendly. Carved on it were two men, one with a blue hood on his head. They were bent over and one was behind the other. This was a bad turn of events, and men said the lot of neither of the figures was good, but that the lot of the one in front was the worse. Then Bjorn made this verse:

(20) The men stand . . .
. . . .
. . . .
. . . .
The hard spear-seeker (man, Thord)
Is fit for this work.
In front stands Thord
Steered by the tree of steel.[20] (man)

Thord thought this thing and its insult ill indeed, and especially that someone should raise this thing on his land. He thought this had been done by Bjorn's hand, and he found little comfort in the poem Bjorn had made. So in the spring he rode to Bjorn's with sixty men and summoned him to the Althing for both the raising of the insult pole and the poem. Their friends, however, talked it over and said they should settle at home rather than bring so ugly a case to the Althing. Bjorn didn't want that so they went to the Thing and settled the case there. Bjorn had to pay three marks of silver for the insult pole raising and the poem. They went home and were more or less at peace for two years so there is nothing to tell of this time.

Chapter 18--Bjorn and the Two Brothers from Vik

In the summer of the third year, during the Althing, a ship landed at Eyrar. Aboard were two brothers from Vik, kinsmen of Thord's. One was named Ottar, the other, Eyvind. They were kinsmen of Thord's on his father's side, and both were very foolhardy men. They sent word to Thord that he should came meet them. They had heard of his good fortune and wanted to come and stay with him. When Thord learned of this he rode south to Eyrar, welcomed his kinsmen, and invited them to his home, and they went home with him. However, not so little had been spoken about Thord and Bjorn that these men hadn't heard about it, and it was commonly thought that Thord had most often come off the worst. These two didn't take to this, for they were very overbearing men, and they said Bjorn wasn't so powerful that one couldn't even the score with him, and they urged Thord not to let matters stand as they were.

The district men often had to travel out to Snaefellness to buy stores of fish and other things, and it so happened at this time that Bjorn went to Saxahval on the shore to his kinsman, Arnor, to buy fish. He was welcomed there, and Thorhild, his foster sister said this to him.

"It is true, Bjorn," she said, "both that you are a powerful man and that you think yourself such. Perhaps I seem outspoken to you, but it seems to me unwise to go against another man with as many enemies as you have. Men have come into the district who aren't often content with second best, and they know Thord has often been worsted by you. It could be that they mean to change that. I have a son here, named Thorfinn, whom I bid go with you even though we can surely feed him well enough at home. I am joyful at your coming, but would be more so were you with twelve men as brave as my son, Thorfinn, or even more than twelve. Everything will be done to help you, but for now you should take less risks with your enemies."

Bjorn said, "Thank you for your good wishes and your offer. I'll take Thorfinn with me, but I don't think there's a need to travel with more."

Bjorn stayed there three nights, and he was treated well. Thord Kolbeinson heard that Bjorn wasn't at home and had gone out to Saxahval, and he then made as though he had business out on the coast and went out to Beruvikhraun with twelve men, among them Ottar and Eyvind, his kinsmen. When they got there Thord told them what the real point of this trip was, that he meant to ambush Bjorn. Thord said he thought Bjorn was soon to leave Saxahval, and he meant to have his life. His kinsmen answered that it was unmanly for twelve men to ambush two. They said they wouldn't have left home with him had they known this, and they gave Thord this choice, to ambush Bjorn himself with only one other man, or to let them, the brothers, do it.

They said, "Though we know Bjorn is a very skilled fighter, we think the man with him will be less skilled than either of us, and that will make up the difference. We would never ambush him with twelve men, though."

Thord said, "Perhaps we should talk about the number of men needed to go against Bjorn after we've been tried, yet I see from this both that you are brave men and that you think yourselves so. Therefore, I'll pick your last choice--you ambush Bjorn. We'll ride away."

They agreed to this.

It is said that Bjorn soon made ready to leave Arnor's. When he did, Arnor's wife came to him and said, "My advice is that you should not cross Beruvikraun with fewer than twelve men. I have dreamed that Thord will ambush you there, for he is shrewd."

"I don't think so," said Bjorn, "if he wanted to ambush me, he would do it nearer his home." Bjorn then left the yard with three others, but after they had been gone only a short time, Thorhild said to her husband, Arnor, "If Bjorn comes to some harm today, then we shall not lie in the same bed tonight." At that, Arnor left home with nine men. He overtook Bjorn on the lava field. Bjorn welcomed him and said, "You have ridden after me quickly, brother-in-law!"

"The reason for that," said Arnor, "is that you seemed slow to ask me, so now I'm inviting myself along."

"So be it," said Bjorn. They dismounted than and led the horses across tha lava field because the loads were too heavy. Bjorn and Arnor went first. Bjorn wore a helmet, held a barbed spear in his hand, and carried a sword at his belt and a shield at his side. Arnor had a spear in hand, and he held a sword in the middle, slung over his shoulder. In this way they started out on the path through the lava field.

The brothers saw that there were more men than they thought Bjorn was likely to have with him, but they felt it would be a bad thing to fall back if it were not Bjorn, so they waited. Suddenly, almost before they were aware of it, Bjorn and Arnor came upon them. Eyvind was the oldest of the two brothers, and he attacked Bjorn. He swung at him with a broad ax, and it hit the helmet and glanced downward. The point struck the shield strap. Bjorn was wounded in the chest and also in the foot. Neither was a great wound. Ottar swung at Arnor's head and cut off his ear and cheek bone. The blow stopped in the sword he had over his shoulder. Bjorn then threw his shield down on the lava field and struck at Eyvind. He gave him his death-blow. Both brothers fell there, and Bjorn made this verse:

(21) The word-hasty woman tyrant
The groom of the cart-horse,
Knows not that I've made
Battle-girded ones to fall. (warriors)
But many battles I've fought,
As my sword bites legs in two.
Unwilling is this glutton
Himself to take me on.

After this the brothers-in-law bound their wounds and buried the two brothers in the lava field. They then outlawed them according to the law for this attack and ambush. Thord Kolbeinson was not far off, and he saw what happened, but it seemed to him not the best moment to attack when there were so many men together. He went home and did nothing further in the matter. He was asked, when he got home, where he'd been so long, and he answered with this verse:

(22) In Hella, in Beruvikhraun,
'Twas the fear of twelve
Sharp, soundless birds (arrows)
That silenced the tear-givers. (warriors)
The vain peacock I saw
Suited in battle-dress,
While off the rocks I ran.
Men wished to get him.

He made still another verse after that:

(23) I know the spike of Baldar's shield*
Thinks his glory greater than mine.
Thinks this wielder of the dragon's lair+
Much too much of himself.
For now the bane of Ull's sword-play**
Has two men cut down.
To the makers of Hogni's squalls++
He would seem better, silenced.

*man--spike of the shield = sword; Balder's sword = man
+man--dragon's lair = gold; gold-wielder = man
**warrior--Ull's sword-play = men; bane of men = warrior
++warriors--Hogni's squalls = battle; makers of battle = warriors

Arnor went home and mended his wounds. Bjorn then left for home, but with more men with him then he came with. One day later on, Bjorn made this verse:

(24) I wish Thord knew--
This battle-maker (warrior, Thord)
I so adore,
Who fled from me
South along the shore--
That before me, alone,
Fell two spear-wielders (warriors)
Fresh meat for ravens.

Bjorn's wounds mended quickly, and it was quiet for a while after this. There was no case taken up for the slain brothers, but Thord had their bodies brought to a church.

Chapter 19--Thorstein's Attack

Kalf the Spiteful lived for some years in Hraundale, as was said before, but after that, it is said that Bjorn rented to him the land at Holm. Bjorn and his father were then living at Voll. Down from Voll is Grettir's lair, and he was living there in a cave that winter when he met Bjorn who had just come to Voll. They often swam together down the river, and were said to be equally strong.[21]

At Voll, Bjorn had a church built and hallowed it for the apostle Thomas, about whom Bjorn also composed a good drápa, or so said Runolf Dalkson. Bjorn had given up his homestead in Holm because he thought he was unable to keep two homes, although he had done so at first for some years since he took over his father's homestead. By now, however, he had enough livestock and was rich enough to keep up two homesteads, so he returned to Holm with his wife, but his mother and Arngeir stayed at Voll.

Up til now Bjorn and Kalf hadn't been very friendly since Kalf had been in with Thord on the ambush. Bjorn thought that Kalf meant to be less than peaceful with him. Now, however, they became friends since Kalf and his son had settled on his land, and they worked the land together.

It is said that later on Kalf the Spiteful bought land west of Hitardalshied. This land was called Selardale. Two farmsteads were there, one called Hurdarbaki. At this farm lived a man called Eid and his two sons, Thord and Thorvald. This farm was next to Kalf's farm in Selardale. In the autumn, after Kalf had moved his household west out of Holm to Selardale, his son Thorstein journeyed south across the moor to Thord's in Hitarness. He was welcomed there, and Thorstein told what had brought him, that he wanted to buy a load of seal meat.

Thor said, "How is it that your friend Bjorn doesn't see to your needs--you who are his good friend?"

Thorstein said, "He has not had a good seal catch."

Thord said, "Have you looked clearly at this friendship of his? I've a hunch he might charge you with something at the Althing in the summer, then get into your hands some stolen goods which you won't find before he has you outlawed. By this will he get that land on which you are settled, and then he will hold all the land as far west of the moor as to the east and south of it."

Thorstein said he hadn't heard of this.

"That's because," said Thord, "you two are dimwitted men, more given to big talk than cleverness, and you won't find it out before he has beaten you out of your land. You've listened to your kinsman, Dalk, and you still want to stick with Bjorn? Dalk and I agree in this matter between you and Bjorn and we want to put Bjorn to death before he has you outlawed. But you, I think, can deal a heavy blow to this, and gain greatly in luck and renown if you thwart this plan by making the first move. You will then get the backing of powerful men."

Thorstein believed this.

Thord said Thorstein should do whatever he asked, adding, "I want nothing for this but your friendship. On your way home, go to Holm and tell Bjorn that you'll be back later to fetch some baren sheep of yours, and don't tell your father about this when you go home."

So Thorstein went away with the seal meat and did as Thord had told him. He went to Holm and told Bjorn he'd be back later for the sheep he and his father kept there. After that, Thorstein went home and brought the seal meat to his father.

Somewhat later, he went south over the moor and got to Holm in the evening when men were sitting at the fire. Thorstein knocked on the door, and Bjorn went to open it. He welcomed Thorstein and bid him stay the night. Thorstein allowed as how he had better go on further, to his kinsman, Dalk's, at Husafell, but he bade Bjorn go with him to the path, adding, "We've go to talk over how I can get my sheep in the morning to drive them home."

Bjorn went out of the yard with him, but he sensed that Thorstein wasn't talking about what was really on his mind because his face was very pale. Bjorn then said he would turn back when they got to the lava field. Thorstein held a sharp wood ax with a long shaft in his hand, but was otherwise lightly clad. It came into Bjorn's mind that Thorstein might have gone to Thord's before he moved to the west. He looked at Thorstein's pale face and he thought maybe Thorstein was a hired killer. Bjorn drew back from him a little and gave him his chance. Thorstein quickly made clear what was on his mind. He raised up the ax to strike at Bjorn's head, but Bjorn ducked under the blow--he knew it was coming-- and grabbed Thorstein around the middle and heaved him way up. At this, Thorstein lost the ax, and it fell down, whereupon Bjorn then threw him to the ground, and none too gently. Thorstein almost died then and there. But Bjorn grabbed him by the throat, then, and strangled him to death. He had no weapons.

Bjorn buried Thorstein there in the lava field and afterwards he went home. His housemen asked where he and Thorstein parted, and Bjorn made this verse:

(25) I know I took the life
Of a warrior, Kalf's son.
Klifsjorva ran with blood.
Into battle went two,
Fearless as they fought,
Though only one held
A weapon of Thund's hail. (battle)
Died that spear of Nid's fire.*

*man--fire of Nid = gold; spear of gold = man

Bjorn slept through the night, but in the morning he got up and went at once with his housemen to where he had buried Thorstein. There he named witnesses and outlawed Thorstein according to the law. Later, Bjorn rode across the moor to Kalf's and offered him atonement for his son. He did so not because he felt he should, but rather for their friendship and since they had settled on his land and still farmed together.

"I know," said Bjorn, "that Thorstein's attack on me was a plot of Thord's."

Kalf said he would take the atonement if he were given self-judgement, but not otherwise. Bjorn said that was not a choice, and that Kalf was being unreasonable to demand anything for an outlawed man, and with that, he rode away.

Because of Thord, Bjorn had now slain three men, none of whom deserved redress under the law.

Chapter 20--Bjorn Overhears a Verse

During the spring, Bjorn went to drive his wethers from below Voll up along the side of the valley where the Husafell farm lay. His housemen were with him, and they saw charcoal smoke rising from a woods and heard men talking. They listened to what was said. Thorkel Dalkson and his houseman were talking about Bjorn and Thord's quarrel and about the verses with which they insulted each other. They disagreed. The houseman sided with Bjorn, but Thorkel with Thord. It had gotten to the point where they were arguing about whose poems were more insulting.

Not long before, Bjorn had made an insult verse about Thord, and by now it was well-known to some. These things were in it: Arnora, Thord's mother, had eaten a "gray-belly" fish she had found on the beach, and from this she had begotten Thord. Thus Thord's parents were not altogether human. So it says in the insult verse:

(26) A fish came up on land
With the tide, on the shore.
A lumpfish he was,
Slime on his skin.
The she-wolf of the cloak (greedy woman)
Ate him, poisoned meat.
Many things there are
Of evil in the sea.

(27) The belly of the bride
Grew below the breast,
So the oak of the dress (woman)
Walked with a lean.
Heavy in the womb,
Too much she'd grown.

(28) A Boy came to light.
The maid had said
To the riches storer (man, Thord's father)
She wished to beget.
But to her it seemed
The dog-biter who came (coward)
Was brave as a goat,
When in his eyes she looked.

The houseman said it now seemed to him that Thord got the worst of it in both verse-making and everything else. He said he hadn't heard a verse as bad as the "gray-belly" insult poem Bjorn had made about Thord. Thorkel then told about a far more insulting cattle-poem Thord had made about Bjorn.[22] The houseman said he'd never heard of it and asked, "Do you know the poem?"

"Sure I know it," said Thorkel, "but it is forbidden to tell it. It was said that anyone who tells it within Bjorn's hearing shall be outlawed."

"Do it for me," said the houseman, "I really want to know, and Bjorn's not around to hear." They argued long. Thorkel refused, but the houseman kept on urging him, saying none were around to hear. At last, Thorkel yielded and recited the poem.

Whereupon Bjorn leaped out at them and said they would have more to do now than recite cattle poems.

"Is it," he said, "that you don't remember that anyone who recites the poem shall be outlawed, or that you just don't care about that?"

Thorkel said he thought Bjorn was eavesdropping in this and he added, "That is not like you, and I don't think you're such a king over men that you can keep men from doing what they want before you." That, he said, he couldn't accept.

Bjorn said, "If I'm not King over other men, I sure am over you!" and struck him his death-blow. The houseman went home and told Dalk the news. He grieved for his son greatly, but there seemed to him little chance for compensation. He had decided before not to meddle in this business between Bjorn and Thord.

Bjorn went home, and for a while after the slaying kept many men with him. Dalk went to meet with Thord Kolbeinson and told him of the slaying and why it was done. Thord felt his own part in this was great and he paid an atonement to Dalk. He would take the case to court if no settlement were forthcoming, but Dalk would have to back him in the suit as best he could.

Later in the spring Dalk sought a settlement with Bjorn. Bjorn was agreeable and didn't refuse to pay an atonement. But Thord began the suit against Bjorn, and when men came to the Thing, Thord pressed the manslaughter charge. However, Bjorn had a defense in this case which was that it had been ruled before that whoever recited this poem within Bjorn's hearing should be outlawed. Bjorn said he overheard Thorkel reciting it, and for that he slew him. They yielded to this defense, and Thord lost the case.

Chapter 21--Bjorn and Kolli

One summer when Kolli the Proud was a youth, Bjorn came to the district Thing. The boy was running around there, only a few years old, but clearly to be the finest of men. Bjorn asked whose son the boy was. A man answered that he was the son of Thord Kolbeinson, and was called Kolli. Bjorn made this verse:

(29) A farer on the fjord's dark horse*
I saw, run up to Gunnur's oak,*
Awful and fearsome in gaze.
Quite a bit like me.
Morn's fire holders say**
The child knows not at all
The Heiti of the traveler++
Of the lobster-rode--his father.

*man/boy--fjord's dark horse = ship; ship farer = man/boy
+man--Gunnur is a valkyrie
**men--Morn's fire = gold; gold holders = men

++man--lobster rode = sea; traveler of the sea = ship; Heiti (a sea god) of the ship = man

Nothing further came up about Kolli's lineage, though Bjorn showed by hinting about it at times that he suspected it were true.

Chapter 22--Bjorn and Thord's Outlaws

One winter, it is said, Bjorn kept some outlaws with him, to do work on the farm. Thord brought suit against Bjorn for this harboring of outlaws. He thought he could get equal for the time when Bjorn had beaten him at law, and as a result now thought himself the victor in lawsuits.

Bjorn answered for himself at the Althing and said he didn't want to deny the charge in this case and wanted to pay atonement for it. The case was then settled, and Bjorn paid the sentence.

Somewhat later, Thord Kolbeinson rescued two outlaws and put them up in Hraundale at Steinolf's. He was married to Thorhalla, Gudbrand's daughter. When Bjorn learned of this, he left home and rode to Steinolf's sheep shed. There he met Erik, the man who lived there in Grjotdale. Bjorn gave him a knife and belt to tell him when those outlaws Steinolf kept left for a ship. He bade him keep watch over them from then on. Thord had meant for them to leave Iceland, and soon he got them some money, for it seemed best to him to get rid of them, and Bjorn had found out about this.

The time came for the outlaws to go to the ship. They got ready in the evening to leave in the night. When Erik found this out, he rode up into Holm and told Bjorn. He set off at once and rode after them. Their route lay across the Hitara river. Bjorn rode hard after them and caught up with them during the night before they crossed the river. In short order, Bjorn slew them both, dragged the bodies under a cliff and buried them. He took the money they had home with him. Thord owned the horses they had used, and late that night Bjorn rode to Thord's with the horses. He got to Hitarness so early that the men were not up yet. There he turned loose the horses used by the outlaws, went up tc Thord and said, "By this I mean to tell you I've slain those outlaws you kept. Now if this angers you, then stand up and avenge them!"

Thord said, "Not without reason were you called a champion."

"What will you give me," Bjorn said, "as a name present?"

Thord said he could have the money he took from the outlaws. At this they parted for the time being and Bjorn rode home. Men said Thord got little honor from all this and that he had gotten the worst of it.

Chapter 23--Two More Verses and a Horsefight

Later on, it is said, Bjorn and Thord held a horsefight near Fagraskagi, and all the district men went to it. There Thord was asked for some amusement, and he didn't refuse. He began to recite a poem he called "Day-Beam" which he had made about Thordis, Bjorn's wife. Bjorn had always called her "Land-Light".[24] Bjorn listened most closely to this entertainment, and he didn't need any asking to answer it. When Thord had finished, Bjorn began to recite a poem he called "Island Candle". When Bjorn had finished, Thord asked his sons, Arnor and Kolli, how they liked this amusement.

Arnor said, "It sure doesn't please me, and it shouldn't be put up with."

Kolli said, "I don't think so, to me it seems equal, one poem against the other."

That was the end of that, and the district men got the amusement they came for. No other great things happened, and nothing had really changed. Thord was no happier than before.

Yet it is said that once the amusement and horsefight were over, Born angrily whipped up another horse with a big horse pole. Thord sat on the back of his horse and rode it around in the ring, waiting for a fight. But when he got to the center of the ring, though, he threw the spear he carried at Bjorn, and it hit his shoulder blade. Bjorn spun around, swing the pole, and he hit Thor's ear, knocking him off his horse. Before anything else happened, men leaped between them and parted them. There the matter rested, and it was quiet for a while.

Chapter 24--Bjorn and the Brothers from Hraunstrand

Some years later, two brothers from Hornstrand came to Thord's in Hitarness for lodging. They stayed the night there, and in the morning they told Thord what their plight was and asked for his help.

Thord said, "For one thing only will I help you."

This happened early in the spring. These brothers' names were Beinir and Hogni, and now they asked this one thing was.

"It may not seem very profitable to you," said Thord, "but I will give you a hundred silvers to take Bjorn's life and bring me his head. I'll give you half now and half when you get back." That was the deal. Thord also promised them his backing. They said they wouldn't fear to attack Bjorn when the chance came.

Later, they went up the valley towards Holm and came to Bjorn's in the afternoon when the cattle were in the milk-pens. They met Thordis, Bjorn's wife, outside the door and asked where Bjorn was. They said they had some business with him. She pointed towards the pasture and said he'd gone there. When she went inside, she told Thordis, Bjorn's mother, about this talk with those men. Bjorn's mother said she thought they were hired killers. When Kolbein, Bjorn's houseman, heard this he grabbed Bjorn's shield and sword and ran with them to where he knew

Bjorn was. He got there first, for he knew the shortest way, and he told Bjorn he thought hired killers were coming to get him.

Bjorn thanked him and then went into the sheep hut with his weapons. The men saw this and followed. When they got to the hut and stopped to think about how to attack him, all of a sudden Bjorn leaped out at them when they least expected it and grabbed both of them by their arms. There was a great difference in prowess between these two and Bjorn. He bound them both, hands behind their backs, but he left their feet free and didn't put them in irons. He then stuck their axes under the ropes on their back and bade them go show themselves to Thord. He took the silver from them and gave it to Kolbein. They went away, and it seemed to them their task had come to ill and shameful to have to return to Hitarness in such a way. Thord said that though they were alive, they could hardly be called men, and he drove them off.

Chapter 25--Bjorn's Return from Thorberg's

There was a woman named Thorberg. Out of friendship she asked Bjorn to her home. He took the offer and stayed with her three nights, well taken care of. The last night he slept restlessly, and when he awoke, the woman of the house asked him what he had dreamed, or what was wrong that he was so restless in his sleep.

He said, "It seemed as if six men were attacking me, and there was great need to defend myself. Maybe that's what caused it."

"It's clear," said Thorberg, "that there are death spirits about who bear you ill. I don't want you to leave here before we find out that no one is going to hinder your journey or wait in ambush for you. Either that or you must leave by a different way, even though it would be somewhat longer, for those who want to get you would guard the shortest and most-used way."

"So is shall be," he said, "I'll go back another way."

He then made ready for the return journey and thanked her well for her kindness to him before they parted. But when he had left the yard, he thought he would go the shorter way. After a while he saw men in front of him at a sheep-pen. He saw it was Thord and his men. There were six altogether. Bjorn made ready to defend himself, if need be. He had on a blue cloak, belted on the outside, and he drew his sword. He had a spear in hand which he threw as soon as he came in range. It went towards a man called Stein, Gudbrand's son, and when it hit him, he died at once. Then a man named Thorbjorn sprang out at Bjorn from among Thord's men, but Bjorn was faster than he was and hit him in the forehead. It was a small wound. Bjorn then swung at Thord, but he took the wisest course and ducked the blow. He was only lightly scratched by it, and when he stood up, Bjorn was no longer attacking him. They parted in this way, and each went home.

Chapter 26--Thord's Ambush

Bjorn's sister lived at Knarrarness, and he went there in the winter and stayed there three days. Each night he had strange dreams. His sister asked him before they parted what they boded for him, and he recited this verse:

(30) Dreamed I now a dream,
Holder of hair land's river fire--*
Still Odin shall make the skald
To feel the fire of swords.
In dream, bloody were my hands,
Reddened in my hand's grasp
Was the great sword Maering,
Bed-fellow to the cold hammer, broken.+

*woman--river fire - gold; hair land = head; holder of the gold of the head (jewelry) = woman
+cold hammer was often used in sharpening old swords

Thord had learned of Bjorn's journey, and with nine men went out to ambush him on the Hitara river. Bjorn left, and on his way home, he saw men on the river bank. He thought it had to be Thord, and he got ready, just as before. He wanted to make a stand, though the odds were greatly against it. When he neared them, they attacked him from all sides. He had no chance for defense and was wounded. He saw then that with things as they were, there was no hope, so he leaped into the river and swam across with his weapons. His shield was across his back. A Norwegian with Thord threw his spear after Bjorn, but it hit the shield. When Bjorn came out of the river, Kolbein, Thord's son, threw his spear across the river and it hit Bjorn in the thigh. Bjorn took this spear and threw it back across the river. It went through one man and hit Thord's son, Kolbein, who was standing behind him. They both died. At this, they left, and Bjorn went on home. His wife nearly fainted when she saw him come home so bloody, and she thought he was gravely hurt, but Bjorn said it wasn't so and that he would get well in a short time.

Thord was not at all pleased.

Chapter 27--Thorstein Kuggason's Journey

There was a man named Thorstein. He was Kuggi's son and lived in Ljarskogi. He was wealthy and well-descended, but was thought to be an overbearing man. He was kin to noble men and good warriors. Thorfinna was his wife. She was a second cousin of Thordis, Bjorn's wife.

Thord Kolbeinson and Dalk called upon Thorstein for help against Bjorn. To get Bjorn seemed to them a hard thing. Thorstein said he wasn't ready for this at the moment, but he added, "It seems to me the best course for you to follow is to make some new charge against Bjorn. That should be easy, for I know he is hardly a man to shun strife. Then will I help your men."

Now Thord thought things were looking up and for Thorstein's friendly promises Dalk bid him come to a Yule feast. He told him to bring as many men as he wished. This all happened in the spring, before the Thing. When men left the Thing in the summer, they watched what they said and didn't hold a district Thing. Men wanted Bjorn and Thord to meet less, not more. So it was now quiet.

The next winter, before Yule, Thorstein got ready for his journey to Dalk's Yule feast. He rode to Strand, to Thorgeir, Stein's son, his kinsman in Breidabolstad. Thorgeir said if he wanted his advice that he shouldn't go on this southern journey, but Thorstein wanted only to go, and he went on with twelve men. His wife, Thorfinna, was with him. She was the daughter of Vermund, from Vatnsfjord. They went to spend the night with Ozur, Kalf's father, and the next day went south to Knappafellsheid and spent the night at Hafrestad in Knappadale. A man called Haf lived there. In the morning they found two ways across Hellisdalshied, one of which goes out of Klifsdale. They went that way, up Hellisdale, then down Klifsdale. This way passes next to Bjorn's farmstead in Holm.

The weather turned bad, and it snowed greatly. Late in the day they came down to one of Bjorn's hay ricks. By then there were great snowdrifts. At the rick was a man who carried the hay out to Bjorn's horses. They greeted him and asked the news.

Thorstein said, "Can you tell us a way across the lava field?"

The houseman said, "I don't think Bjorn's housemen have to reward you with friendship, and I'll not do that."

Thorstein said, "Perhaps if you were made to go with us, you would think better of this."

"You can do that," said the houseman, "if you wish."

The weather worsened both from the drifting snow and the cold, and the houseman got away before they noticed. He went home and told Bjorn he'd just gotten out of a fix. He said Thorstein Kuggason and twelve men had just come upon him and tried to force him to be a guide.

Bjorn said, "If Thorstein is as wise as he is hard and eager, then he shall come here in the evening and not risk himself where he is now. But if he goes up into the dale against the weather or down across the lava field, the streams and other hard places, then he will not fare well. I'll bet that he'll be here in the evening."

Thorfinna rode, but the men walked, and they were worn out because they had been on the heath, and now they saw that the houseman had escaped. They talked among themselves about what course to take, but the weather only worsened and the dark night fell on them. Thorfinna said, "If it's any harder for you, Thorstein, to hang on to Bjorn than his houseman--and he's a far greater man-- then this business of yours is not likely to go well. I know you think you should be against Bjorn, but it seems wise to me to keep in mind our bonds with Thordis, my second cousin, and not very wise to risk our lives here outside Bjorn's farm. That is less manly than to put ourselves wholly in his hands. So let's go to him. If we seek him out at home, we'll be welcomed, if he's a good man."

Thorstein was very unwilling to do this and he started out again. A little while later, they saw a man standing beside another another of Bjorn's hay ricks. It was Sigmund, a houseman of Bjorn's. Thorstein bade him point out the way down to Husafell.

He said, "I'm hardly able to show men the way in drifting snow and the dark of night." But at last he mounted the back of Hviting and rode along with them, following Thorfinna. They came to the Hitara river, but this had swollen greatly, and they got very wet from it. Then Thorstein got a hunch about the way they were going, and it was as he thought. They were on the way to Holm, where Bjorn was, and thirty fighting men with him. Thorstein and his men had a hard time of it, for the way to the farmstead was not short. The house stood below Holmsfjall. Bjorn's houseman rode into the yard in front of everyone. When they got to the house and knocked at the door, Bjorn told this houseman, who's been sent to the hay rick, to go back and bid Thorstein, if it was he, to stay here.

"But I should guess," said Bjorn, "that to him you will seem of little importance, and hardly able to supply a good welcome, for men say truly that only he makes an offer who can do so. But you tell him that he must either trust your offer or else go away."

So the houseman did as he was told, and it went as Bjorn had guessed. Thorstein said he wouldn't accept an offer from him. He said he must be asked by the owner. The houseman bade him take this offer or go away.

Thorstein took the offer because he didn't see how they could get to another farm if they left. When they came in, they were greeted and set to table. No fire was made, however, nor were their clothes set out, and they were wet and frosty.

Bjorn asked the news, but coldly and with little interest. But his wife offered Thorfinna a good welcome. Thorstein began to think maybe they should leave during the night. It seemed all he'd gotten was cold-heartedness. But Bjorn had said no man could lead them in the drifting snow and darkness, and that it wasn't too hard to give them a welcome for the night. Their shoes and socks were ice-covered, and they couldn't get out of them because no fire was made, but cloaks were put over them. The were not offered dry clothes. They got only cheese and curds for the night meal, though at that time the fast hadn't been taken into the law.

Bjorn asked Thorstein, "How do men call such a meal in your district?"

He answered and said men call it cheese and curds.

Bjorn said, "We call it an unfriendly welcome."

They then took their night's rest by pulling off their pants and stockings and hanging them, stiff with frost, on planks. Then they lay down to sleep. In the morning Bjorn got up quickly and looked at the weather. When he came back inside, he shut the door behind him. Thorstein asked what the weather was like. Bjorn said it was good weather for bold men. Thorstein called to his men and bade them make ready, and they did so. Thorfinna was taken to a seat in the sitting room. When Thorstein went outside, he saw the weather was awful.

He said, "Bjorn surely didn't give us nice weather to go in, but then he doesn't know what shape we're in."

Bjorn heard what he said and answered, "Even a beggar would start for Husafell in weather like this."

Thorstein grew furious under this prodding and left for the sitting room where he found Thorfinna. There was another woman with her. Few words were spoken. Bjorn also came in. A great frost had followed the snowstorm, and for a while now the skies were clear.

Bjorn said, "I'll give you this choice. Either you stay here for the four days of Yule--and you'll get the best welcome I can give you--or, those of you who want to can leave. Thorfinna, however, should stay back, and also those who are frost-bitten."

Thorstein said he didn't want to lose his men, and he said it might be better if they stayed, so he chose that.

"Good," said Bjorn, "you made the wiser choice."

Whereupon Bjorn had a great fire built and bade Thorstein warm himself and dry his clothes. Thorfinna urged Thorstein to accept from Bjorn all that he now offered, and she added, "We shall not be shunned hereafter, and we should excuse his coldness at first. There is also better honor for both of you in treating each other well."

Thorstein willingly agreed to this and moved up to the fire with his men. Bjorn was now very cheerful, and he said, "It so happened that you were forced to come here, but I was so cold to you the first night because I wanted there to be other talk in Husafell than that I was trying to make friends with you. From now on, however, I shall host you as best I can."

Now the best of welcomes was given them, and Mass was sung the next day of Yule. They stayed there the four nights of Yule and accepted the warm welcome offered them.

By now the storm had cleared up. Thorstein bade his men get ready, and they did so. Bjorn sent for one of his studhorses, which were fed near the hay-rick during the storm. This horse was the offspring of Hviting, and he was all white in color, though the mare had been brown. Another of Hviting's offspring was in Thorarinsdale. He was also white even though the mare had been black. Bjorn had this first horse brought to Thorstein and said he wished to give it to him.

Thorstein said he didn't want to accept it yet, and he added, "because I have done nothing for the gift. And if I cannot reward you for this good welcome I've accepted, it is unlikely I can reward you for any more that you do for me. But if I can repay you worthily for the good welcome, then I will accept the horse and see that the gift will in some worthy way be rewarded. So, I shall now offer to be a peace-maker between you and Thord. The matter can't rest as it is. Though the men you've laid to rest were unworthy, and though you've acted within the law, you will still have a run-in with Thord unless someone makes the peace in this case. Now I'll tell you what I'm going to do. You must pay some money for each of them, though it will be less than what they want. The difference I will pay, and then they will think they have come off well in the matter."

Bjorn said, "I agree to this, and I put it all in your hands."

"So now," said Thorstein, "I will undertake to do this." Bjorn followed them to the gate.

There were four horses, all told, which he gave to Thorstein.

Chapter 28--Thorstein Talks to Thord

Thorstein and his men then went to Husafell. Many men were already there, and so was Thord Kolbeinson. The feast was a good one. Thord welcomed Thorstein, though he was less friendly than he'd been before Thorstein had stayed as Bjorn's guest. After the eighth day of Yule Thord took Thorstein and his men home with him to Hitarness, and they stayed there the rest of Yule. After Yule, Thorstein asked Thord if he would trust him to make the peace in this case with Bjorn. He said Bjorn had agreed to it. Thord said that seemed promising, but he added, "It still seems strange to me, though, that you stayed with Bjorn during the storm."

Thorstein said it hadn't seemed very promising to venture out in such harsh weather and bring harm to himself and his men. Thorstein spoke to Dalk about the settlement before he left, and Dalk was not unwilling that Thorstein should handle the matter, so then Thorstein brought up the matter even more often with Thord, but Thord was still much more unwilling than Dalk. Thorstein said men would say they had named a good peace-maker if he took up the case, and he said his friendship with Bjorn was still young. Finally, due to Thorstein's urging, they decided to do it, and Thord and all the rest agreed to Thorstein's handling the case.

Chapter 29--The Last Two Verses

It is said that the peace meeting was held at a farmstead below Hraun. Bjorn was sent for, and he came with his men while Thord stayed inside. Thorstein acted as peace-maker. After they had talked for a while and brought up the settlement, things were looking more good than not under Thorstein's handling.

Then Thord said, "There is still something not quite clear about the settlement."

Thorstein asked what that was.

Thord said, "It's Bjorn's and my insult poems. We haven't talked about that, and now I want both of us to recite all the poems we've each made about each other."

Thorstein said that would be uncalled for.

"Not at all," said Thord, "I want to know who has made the most poems. I do not mean to be bested in this by Bjorn."

So it went as Thord had asked. Each of them recited all the peoms they had made about each other. This was amusement worth hearing only to some. It turned out that Bjorn had made one more than Thord, and Thord said he wanted to make a poem to counter it. Thorstein said that was uncalled for, and so did many others. Bjorn answered and said he didn't want to be blamed for the poem. He said he would let Thord make another poem, but he added, "If you won't let this pass, then delay no longer, but don't let clear insult be in it."

Thorstein said he was little honored by Thord and his people when they wished in this way not to hold to the settlement he had made. He said he could do little more in this case. Thord said he didn't care whether Bjorn allowed it or not, and he made this verse:

(31) With the rising dawn
Of each passing day,
Is Bjorn dishonored more.
At all insult, the idiot yawns.
The hated boaster, full of fear,
Who lacks all truth and sense,
Sits fast on his buttocks.
May he never thrive!

"You can hear by that," said Bjorn, "that this scoundrel wants no settlement. This poem shall not go unrewarded either!" Bjorn made this verse:

(32) Thord, that you're better I deny,
And a verse I will not owe.
Craven braggart, with no skill,
Never have verses hurt you more,
Than the last I made for you,

Holder of the ice of terror.*
In great folly that one led you.+
Now I've made the ale of Odin.**

*man--ice of terror = sword; sword-holder = man
+it prompted Thord to break the settlement
**Odin's ale = poetry, a verse

The settlement had come to this end, and the men now left the Thing. Thorstein went to Hitarness with Thord and stayed there a little while. When he left, he got no great gifts from Thord. It seemed to Thorstein Thord's actions had marred the settlement, and their friendship was dwindling. He thought his counsel had been little honored in this case.

Thorstein then went to Bjorn's in Holm and stayed there a while. When he left, Bjorn went with him as far as Hitardalshied, and before they parted there they had a frank and sincere talk. Bjorn said he accepted Thorstein's judgment. He said, "We have become friends. I want to keep this friendship and remain your friend. Now both of us have some enemies, and I would like to pledge that if one of us dies from either weapons or men's hands, the other avenge him."

Thorstein said he felt pledged to at least as much when he offered his friendship, and he added, "But we should also say something about the revenge, since now men know better than before what should be done. I want to say that each of us should take self-judgment for the other and get money or outlawry or a money settlement rather than kill in return. There is more honor in that for Christian men."

Whereupon they firmly agreed that each of them would avenge the other or take up the case at law, as if they were brothers born of the same parents. At this, Bjorn had the studhorses led forth again, and Thorstein agreed now. He said that he wanted to accept each and every one. The horses were to remain there that winter and the following summer, but after that, Bjorn would send them west in the autumn. Thorfinna gave Bjorn a gold ring and a velvet waistband which King Olaf had given Thord Kolbeinson, but which the King had awarded to Bjorn after the robbery in Brenney island. With this, they parted good friends and went home.

A little while later Bjorn got an eye sickness. It hurt for some time, and although he got better after a while, his eyes grew weaker, and dimmed, and he was not as clear-sighted as before.

It seemed to men now that hope for peace between Bjorn and Thord was lost. Thord and the men who had sided with him in the case were greatly angered. Bjorn and Thorstein Kuggason, however, had become fast friends.

Chapter 30--Thord Gathers His Men

The winter passed and the following summer, and things between Bjorn and Thord were more or less quiet. In the autumn, Thorfinn Thvarason went out to Ness to his father's with fifteen men. He had Bjorn's sword, Maering, and Bjorn had his weapon. Bjorn was home with few men. Some of his housemen had gone to the public sheep-pen in Laugavatnsdale, and some had gone other places. Thord and Kalf waited at Hitarness with many men. They meant, if the chance came, to burn Bjorn inside his home. Bjorn didn't know this.

Arngeir, Bjorn's father, wanted to see some kinfolk in Knarrarness, and when he left in the morning, he took the weapons Bjorn kept at home with him. Bjorn had gone to see the horses.

Arngeir took the wrong way, but didn't discover it before he came upon Thord's barn at Hitarness. He met a cow-hand who told him to get away at once, but there were women in the barn, and they could not keep secret about Arngeir's coming when they got back to the house. When Thord, Kalf, and Dalk found this out, they figured few men were with Bjorn at home, and while they talked over their plans, Thord made this verse:

(33) To all mighty war spirits
Who shaped the skies,
I pray, and all battle-gods.
'Tis right the bloody eagle
Stands with reddened beak

Over headless Bjorn,
Swayer of steel's song.*
While I in victory stand.

*man--steel's song = battle; swayer of battle = man

Now Kalf strongly urged that they slay Bjorn, if they could. He said he had long been ready to fight Bjorn, even though he was stronger then than he is now. Dalk answered that it was best to use this chance, when Bjorn had few men. He said it would be no small matter to fight Bjorn, but that Bjorn's high-handedness would no longer hang over their heads in this case, if one took revenge. He said Thord should take charge of this scheme and lead.

"The rest of us," he said, "will follow you."

Whereupon they agreed that Kalf go to Hurdarbak for the sons of Eid, Thorvald and Thord, and tell him of Thord Kolbeinson's plan and what they were about to do. Those two broke away quickly and went with Kalf. Their way took them across the Thorarinsdalsa river in Hiterdale, and there they met one of Bjorn's housemaids who was on her way to Voll. They asked her the news out of Holm, what men were doing there and how many were home with Bjorn. She was not short of words and told them much. She said there were three other men home besides Bjorn, and they were in the forest chopping wood. At this, they left her, and as fast as they could, went to find Thord and Dalk to make ready for the attack on Bjorn.

There were twenty-four who went. Among them was Kolli, Thord's son. From the afternoon to the evening they went below Hraun and later in the night on that path which lies in the valley above Voll until they reached the land at Holm. There they talked with each other, and Thord laid out the way to get Bjorn. Then they all pledged themselves to this agreement, that if Bjorn were killed and atonement demanded, they would all pay money, but chiefly Thord, Dalk, or Kalf, whichever of them was his slayer. That day there was to be a public sheep roundup in Thorinsdale and one in upper Hitardale as well.

Chapter 31--The Plan

After this, Thord set things up. When morning came, he had Kalf go back to the path to Voll which they had ridden on in the night. With him were six men, and they were to ambush Bjorn, should he come that way. But Eid's sons, Thord and Thorvald, and Kolli, Thord's son, were to lie in wait on the way to Hvitingshjalli, should Bjorn come that way. There were pastured those horses which Bjorn had given Thorstein, and often Bjorn went to see to them. Hvitingshjalli was named after the older Hviting. However, Dalk, from Husafell, was to wait for him on the way which goes to the mountains on the east side of the lake. He was to watch for him there because they thought it unlikely Bjorn would go up the valley to a sheep roundup when so few men were at home. Thord was to wait on the way which goes from Holm down to Husafell. Thord figured Bjorn would go to one or the other of the sheep roundups, and he thought it more likely he would go to Thorarinsdale, for more of his sheep would be there. So Thord waited there, in case he came that way. There were six men in each ambush. They had covered all the ways they thought Bjorn might use in leaving, but they didn't want to go into Holm before it were known for sure that Bjorn had left. They felt it was too hard to attack him at home. So they parted then, and each went to those spots where they would wait for Bjorn.

Chapter 32--The Attack

It is said that while this was going on, Bjorn got up early that morning and ate. Sigmund, his houseman, had gone visiting up in the valley, and Bjorn thought ill of these visits of Sigmund while he still had enemies, for he believed it wasn't out of the question that he might need a man. So now he was frowning when he told Thordis, his wife, that he was going to Hvitingshjalli to trim the manes of Thorstein's horses before he sent them west. He also said he'd had a rather bad dream in the night, and was unsure what it meant. He said he'd often had the same kind of dream, but that it had never before been so bad.

She said, "I don't want you to leave the house today. You're not being careful, and you may have enemies waiting all around for you. What did you dream?"

"I'll not let the dreams keep me from going," he said.

Thordis answered, "I so not want you to leave the house, and I want you to be most careful. That, at least, has never hurt anyone. Still, it seems to me you really must have had a bad dream last night. Tell me what it was."

Bjorn made this verse:

(34) Strange t'would be were not
My guardian spirit warning me--
Long awake have I lain
When of this hatred I heard--
When the helmed goddess*
Of the arm serpents
Of the day's fire ruler+
Each dream bids home the skald.

*valkyrie--arm serpents = rings; goddess of rings = woman; helmed woman = valkyrie
+God--day's fire - sun; ruler of the sun = God; thus God's valkyrie, Bjorn's guardian spirit.

"This I have often dreamed," he said, "but most vividly last night."

Thordis tried to keep him from leaving the house, but he wouldn't be stopped. The housemen who were left at home went out to cut wood, and Bjorn was now the only man of age left. He made ready to go see to the horses. He had a great pair of mane scissors on his belt and a hood on his head, and a shield by his side. He held Thorfinn Thvarason's sword in hand.

Bjorn was a very large man. He was handsome, with many freckles, a red beard, and curly hair, and though dim of sight, still the best of fighters. A boy of fifteen went with him, and when they had crossed the home meadow, Bjorn spoke this verse:

(35) With a little band I leave,
Not much have I to fight
A fierce attack of vengeance--
Sword only, and white shield.
But before through Myra I yield,
To a lone sea-beast ruler,*
Yet shall my hilted wand (sword)
Widely swing in my hand.

*warrior--sea-beast = ship; shipruler = warrior

They went on the way towards Hvitingshjalli. They had to cross the Hitara river a short way from the point where it came out of the lake. When they had gone on for a while, the boy saw six men coming at them from the hay-rick at Hvitingshjalli. Bjorn asked the boy if he could see the horses on the hillside. He said his eyesight was of little use. The boy said he saw the horses, and also six men coming at them. Bjorn then spoke this verse:

(36) Two battle-wards are we,
But in truth are we more,
For oft was this skald
At the feast of the wolf.
Came west in the autumn
A stout-hearted man.
Not little then was the fine band
Of this brave hord-breaker. (Bjorn)

Bjorn wore a fine jacket, and he had a silk ribbon wrapped around his leg thongs, the ones he had exchanged with King Olaf the Holy. He drew Thorfinn Thvarason's sword and said, "A bad sword has here a good swordsman!"

Soon Kalf saw them, from where he was waiting. He turned after them and said, "Luck is hardly against us! Thord and his men thought to put me in the place it was least likely Bjorn would go, but I think I shall now catch that bear we all want."

"They will shortly be here, Bjorn," said the boy, "for they're coming fast!"

Bjorn answered, "It will be easier, then, to catch the horses--with more help."

The boy said, "These aren't peaceful men. They're all armed--and I see still more armed men coming after us."

"Don't worry much about that," said Bjorn, "it could be that those are the men from the sheep round-up."

The boy said, "I see still more men, and they're coming from Holm! The only thing for us to do is to turn towards Hellisdale. If we can then get to Klifsdale, we're safe."

Bjorn said, "Up till now, I've never fled, and so it still will be. I shall not turn back. We shall go along Klifsandi to Klifsjorva. I very much want to see Grastein the Large, if we can get there."

"I don't know," said the boy, "how it will end for us. Men are attacking us from all sides, and I now clearly see they're in groups of six, though some are farther away from us then others. No less than twenty-four men do I see now!"

Bjorn asked, "Where are the men nearest us?"

The boy told him and Bjorn thought he recognized Kalf from what he said. Kalf was tall and dark and was now a short way from their backs. Kolli and Eid's sons were coming from their front, and Dalk and his men were coming up from Holm. They were the farthest away.

Bjorn said to the boy, "You go up on the hillside, now, after the horses. I will wait here. It's no use to go further."

Bjorn sat down then, and the boy went to catch the horses. He wanted to come back, but he couldn't because by then the fight had begun.

The first to come at Bjorn were Kalf and his six men along with Kolli and Eid's sons and their men, another six. Thorvald, Eid's son, threw a spear at Bjorn as soon as he got near enough, Bjorn grabbed the spear out of the air and sent it back to its owner. It hit Thorvald in the belly and he fell to the ground, dead. They had now gotten between Bjorn and Grastein's, so Bjorn was cut off.

Thord wanted to avenge his brother and swung a great blow at Bjorn. Bjorn held the shield with his arm in the hand-grip, but the blow hit the shield so hard that Bjorn's hand-grip broke apart and the shield fell down. At this, Bjorn grabbed the pointed end of the shield and drove it into Thord's head so that he died at once. Some men say, though, Bjorn killed him with a short sword.

Kolli attacked Bjorn hard, very nearly the hardest of all the men there, though we do not know what wounds he gave him.

Kalf said it mattered not to him that Bjorn had killed some of their men. He said he wouldn't fail this time, and he added, "We're hardly lacking men!"

Some said they should form a ring around Bjorn to keep him from escaping and wait for Thord Kolbeinson to put an end to him. While they were talking about this, Bjorn freed the mane shears from his belt. He had just sharpened them before he left home, and they were large and sharp.

At this point Dalk came up with six men. He wanted to attack Bjorn at once, because he was a bold fighter and thought it hardly necessary to have a formal duel with Bjorn, when he had a son to avenge.

But Bjorn Then drew Thorfinn's sword, the one he'd brought from home, and struck Dalk's leg so hard it broke, though the sword didn't cut it. Dalk could do no more, and he fled to safety.

At this point, Thord Kolbeinson came up--at last--and when Bjorn saw him he said, "Slow in coming, little boy."

"Yet, so near you will I stand today," said Thord, "that I will swing a low blow at you."

"That shall you only swing," said Bjorn, "while you live!"

Thord had made a slip of the tongue. He had wanted to say he would give Bjorn a shame stroke.[25]

Bjorn now grabbed the shears, for he knew the sword was useless, and leaped at Thord, meaning to drive the shears into him. Thord ducked the blow, and it hit Grim, Thord's houseman. He died at once.

At that moment, Kalf swung at Bjorn and gave him a great wound. Bjorn fell to his knees, then, and defended himself with the shears. He fought with great heart, for he was the bravest of men, as had often been proved, but his attackers gave him many wounds, and came at him now in a frenzy. None more so than Kolli.

Bjorn said, "You're attacking me hard today, Kolli."

"I'm not given to mercy," said Kolli.

"So also," said Bjorn "will your mother charge you with attacking me the hardest. It's quite clear your gifts lie elsewhere than in knowledge of where you come from!"

Kolli said, "I don't remember you saying that earlier--that I am kin to you." Nevertheless, Kolli went away at once, and stopped his attack.

Bjorn defended himself a very long time with the shears, on his knees. Men wondered why he put up such a defense, a nearly weaponless man, against so many. It seemed that anyone who got near him had a hard time of it.

At last, it is said, Thord swung at Bjorn and cut off his buttocks. At this, Bjorn fell. Thord wasted no time with the death-blow, and with another stroke, he cut off Bjorn's head. Then Thord spoke this verse:

(37) So has it fallen out
Battle-brave man--
Sword Edges bit him
Who challenged me
On the south heath--
This man has robbed me;
In justice bit this sword.

Thord bound Bjorn's head with straps and let it hang from his saddle. Kalf said he wanted to go to Holm and make the slaying known. He said he wanted to bring them the necklace Bjorn had worn. Dalk answered that such was not fitting and would provoke them. He said there was more honor in showing themselves willing to pay Bjorn's kinsmen rather than making it worse by doing such a thing. Thord stayed out of this. Kalf then left the site of the battle with Thord, and when they had ridden for a while and come down across Klifsand, some ravens flew towards them. Thord made this verse:

(38) Ravens, where race you,
Fast with a black flock?
Food you should be seeking
Northeast of Klifsand
It's there Bjorn lies,
Over him, the blood-geese. (carrion birds)
Above Hvitingshjalli
Fell the helmet holder.

Chapter 33--Thord Makes Known the Slaying

So they went to Holm, and Kalf went into the room where Thordis, Bjorn's wife, was. He told her of Bjorn's slaying.

"Here is the necklace," he said, "which he was wearing. It's for you!"

She took the necklace and asked if Thord was there. Kalf said he was.

"I wish to speak to him," she said, and went out of the room to where Thord was waiting. She threw the necklace at him and bade him take it to Oddny, his wife, as a keepsake.

After this, they rode down the valley and came to Husafell. Dalk stayed there, but Thord rode on to Voll. Arngeir, Bjorn's father, had just come home. Thord told the news to both man and wife. She was outside, washing the head of a child.

Thord untied Bjorn's head from the straps and he threw it at Thordis, Bjorn's mother. He bade her see if she knew the head, and he said there was no less need to wash this head than the one she had been washing.

Whereupon Thordis said, "I know this head, and so should you, because before that same head you often trembled when it was on its body! Go now, and take it to Oddny. It will seem better to her than that wretched little head which dangles from your neck!"

Thord was not pleased with her words. He let Bjorn's head stay there, and he rode home to Hitarness. There he told everyone what had happened, and he brought Bjorn's necklace to Oddny. When she saw it, she fell down in a faint, and when she came to, she fell ill with a heavy brooding. Thord sought many times to be gentle and comfort her, but she worsened until she was greatly sick from this. She became even worse in the winter.

The only thing that helped her was to sit on horseback while Thord led the animal to and fro. This he did because her illness hurt him deeply, and he wanted to comfort her. About this he made a verse:

(39) Weary am I these many days,
Frid's fair cloth on horse to lead.*
The journey of this ailing woman
Is not easy, nor swiftly ridden.
the Hlokk of the pool's shining+
Finds nowhere ease for care.
To this sword of Modi**
A great sorrow it is.

*woman--Frid = goddess; cloth of goddess = woman
*woman--pool's shining = gold; Hlokk (valkyrie) of gold = woman
*warrior--Modi = Thor's son

So greatly did Thord grieve over his wife's illness that men said he would rather choose Bjorn's fate, were that possible, to regain his wife's love. He thought it a great sorrow that Bjorn's and his and Oddny's path had ever crossed.

Oddny went on grieving and withered away. Though she lived much longer, joy never returned to her.

Bjorn's kinsmen saw to his body and had it buried at Voll by the church he had built there for the Apostle Thomas. He was laid to rest in the clothes and leg thongs as was told before.

Chapter 34--The Settlement

The news of Bjorn's slaying spread widely through the land. Bjorn's brother, Asgrim, who lived east in Rangarvoll heard of it, and he went west to Ljarskogr to find Thorstein Kuggason. Thorstein took the case from old Arngeir, and in the spring they all made ready for the Althing, Thorstein, Asgrim, and Bjorn's friends.

When Asgrim left Thorstein in the winter, he went to Holm and took under his care Bjorn's farmstead. He went from there in the spring with Thorstein and a great many men to the Thing to make ready the suit. Thord and his backers also came.

It is said that when Thord got to the Thing, he sent men secretly to Asgrim to make him a handsome offer. They asked him to a night meeting and they said they would allow him the most honor from this suit. They said that was only fitting since he himself was never against them in their dealings with Bjorn.

Asgrim wasn't used to dealing with lawsuits, and he met with Thord in the night. They talked a great deal about it, and Thord talked to Asgrim winningly. Thord was a master of words and smooth talk, and he showed Asgrim how greatly he was forced into doing what he did. Thord told him all about his dealings with Bjorn and about how he had always come off worse than Bjorn, and how even now he had three of his men slain in the last meeting with Bjorn, and four wounded.

"And there are twelve men," he said, "for whom there is no settlement! Ottar and Eyvind, Thorstein Kalfson, Thorkel Dalkson, two outlaws, Stein Gudbrandson, and the eighth is a Norweigen. The nineth is my son, Kolbein, then Thorvald and Thord Eidson, and the twelfth is my houseman, Grim. Also, Dalk is badly wounded, and all of us have some wounds. I shall now pay three hundred silvers for your brother, because I want you to come off well."

Asgrim listened to Thord's argument and agreed to this. Thord gave him the silver and he took it. All this was done rather quickly. It was clear what caused this settlement--Thord's smooth talking and Asgrim's rashness.

Thorfinn Thvarason no sooner became aware that Asgrim had taken the money than he left the booth to find Thorstein Kuggason. He told Thorstein that Asgrim had been fooled into settling with Thord in secret. He said he was at that moment counting silver. Thorstein said this was indeed a rash deed, and that it was not easy to help such self-willed men, and he added, "But it's still hard to figure how Thord got this done."

No one had the slightest inkling that Asgrim would ask no one's, not even Thorstein's advice, and Thorstein was his partner in the case. Thorstein and Asgrim were bringing forward the case of Bjorn's death because the one who was the closest to Bjorn, his father, old Arngeir, was now infirm with age. He let them handle the case because he felt that due to his age he wouldn't be able to go to the Thing. Besides, he didn't have much to do with lawsuits when he was younger, and he knew Thorstein had promised Bjorn to take up the case for him, that if need be, the one who lived the longest would take up the case for the other.

Thorstein now sent men to the booth of his kinsman, Thorkel Eyjolfson, to say he wished to meet with him. Thord Kolbeinson had been in Thorkel's booth when he made the settlement with Asgrim. He made it without Thorkel's leave. Thorkel didn't know about it.

It is said that then Thorstein got together a great band of men, and also called the Myramen, Bjorn's kinsmen. Then he and Thorkel met. With Thorstein were all Bjorn's kinsmen and friends. Thorstein said he was bound by a promise either to avenge Bjorn or to take up his suit, and he added, "We are all now gathered here, his kinsmen and friends, to say that we are all of one mind to strike down the settlement Asgrim made with Thord."

"Often has it seemed," said Thorkel, "that Bjorn's kinsmen have not followed the right in these matters. So I'm not surprised that men should fix it so the one with legal right in this case can't keep the settlement which pleases him."

"We're not here to talk about it," said Thorstein, "I only want to end the case in outlawry or atonement, as I am bound to do, or else lose my life. Don't stand against us if you don't want to settle this in battle. We have enough men, and it's unlikely those who oppose us would win. We would then give them a choice. Either we take Thord's life, or the lives of others who slew Bjorn."

Thorkel and Thorstein were first cousins, and Thorkel saw it befitted him not to go on with this and surely come to blows with Thorstein, and after all, Thord had not talked over the settlement with him. He wanted the case to go in Thord's favor, but he didn't want to go into battle with his kinsmen for Thord's sake. He said he wanted Thord not to be outlawed and not to have to pay more than he already had, but that Thorstein could hit the other men at the slaying with as much money and outlawry as he wanted. Thorstein said it wasn't right that Thord escape penalty, since from him had all the evil come in this case.

Thorkel said, "I wish then that money be used to settle this case. We set forth and agree that Thord will escape outlawry with a money penalty."

The case then came to the point where peace-makers were named, and it was settled with them that Thorstein and Thorkel should make the judgment, and that Thord was to pay as his penalty whatever Thorstein wished. The other men at the slaying were to undergo both outlawry and money penalty, as Thorstein saw fit. All were to pay the money before leaving the Thing, and so it was done.

It was quite fitting that Thorstein alone give out the penalties, since his kinsmen, Thorkel, had just gotten Thord out of an outlawry penalty. Thorstein wasn't sparing in his judgment, for there was enough money around.

This was the judgment of Thorstein and his men: Dalk was to get no money for himself or his son, but neither was he to pay for his part in Bjorn's slaying. Kalf also was to get no money for his son. He was to be outlawed from the district. He would lose his land in Selardale, and must go south across the moor to his birthplace. Asgrim was to keep the three hundred silvers Thord had already paid him, and Thord was to pay another three hundred to escape outlawry, and yet another for Kalf's freedom. Thord's kinsmen who fell on the lava field fell unhallowed, and were thus outlaws, as well as all the men who had been in on Bjorn's ambush. There were twelve men left who had actually been at the slaying, and Thorstein condemned them to outlawry. They must leave Iceland that same summer, and were to be given money for passage, a mark for each of them. If they didn't leave, as the sentence ordered, they would be held outlaws of the worst sort and slain wherever they were found.

With this, they left the Thing. Thorkel, however, chose to let the kinsmen of the outlawed men raise money to help them leave Iceland in the summer.

It was the talk of men that scarcely ever had such a settlement been made for a single man as had been made for Bjorn. All agreed that what Thorstein sentenced should be carried out. Thord and his men thought it very bad indeed, though they could do nothing about it. The Myramen who were Bjorn's kinsmen also got a great deal of money from Thord Kolbeinson in the settlement. Old Arngeir took a lot of money to Thorstein Kuggason which he accepted, and Thordis took out her bride-price and dowery and went west towards Bardastrand to her kinsmen in Breidafjord. Asgrim want east to Rangarvoll with the money he was alloted, and lived there afterwards. Thord Kolbeinson went home to his farm at Hitarness, and was not pleased with the outcome of the case. The matter settled down after this, and here ends this saga.

Notes on the Saga of Bjorn, Champion of Hitardale

[1]The nickname means Island Candle.

[2]Early Icelandic marriages required the paying of a stipulated amount, the "bride-price," to legalize the marriage. This amount was paid by the bridegroom, and on the wedding night became the personal property of the bride.

[3]A *drápa* is a long, formal praise poem with a refrain.

[4]The custom of gift giving at Yule was a fairly common practice of early Germanic rulers. It may have been borrowed in the earliest times from the Romans.

[5]King Valdimar (Vladimir) the Great ruled Russia from 980-1015.

[6]By "eastern lands" is probably meant eastern Europe and western Russia.

[7]The last three lines of this poem have been freely adapted. the actual text of the poem at this point states that Bjorn is "very near" her at the moment in a tent with four men. The narrative, however, clearly places Bjorn in Russia, not Iceland, at this point.

[8]Small islands off the coast of Sweden near the mouth of the Gaut Elf River, much used by trading ships of the time.

[9]The saga probably confuses Skuli with his father, Thorstein, here. By this time Thorstein, an old man, has likely died, and it is said in Egil's saga that Skuli, not an old man at this point in *Bjarnar saga*, lived to an old age. Also, the man referred to here as Bjorn's foster-father must be someone other than Skuli who fostered Bjorn before Skuli. His identity was likely made known in the lost original beginning of the saga.

[10]Probably Thord's men, the ones present at the meeting of Bjorn and Thord on Brenney Island.

[11]An obscure passage. Olaf probably finds it just that Thord's men got at least their money in his judgement because they later supported the truth of Bjorn's story, while all Thord got was freedom from Bjorn's persecution.

[12]Ingjald is mentioned only here in the saga. Possibly he is identified more fully in the lost original beginning of the saga. He may be the unidentified foster father of Bjorn.

[13]In none of the MSS is the name spelled out. It may have been "Vigi" (fighter). At least that was the name of a famous dog owned by Olaf Tryggvason.

[14]A proverbial saying, though its use in this context is somewhat obscure. Thord probably means any promises of friendship he may recently have extended to Bjorn do not cancel all the preexisting enmity.

[15]Solundir are islands off Sogni, in Norway, but the narrative reports the action to have taken place on the Brenney islands. In all likelihood oral tradition supported the location given in the verse, and the author of the narrative, apparently, made no attempt to resolve the contradiction.

[16]This verse is very similar to a verse in _Eyrbyggja_ saga, (28), attributable to Bjorn Bredvikingakappi. This similarity could be the result of imitation or both verses could have been merely variants in the oral tradition.

[17]At this point there is a lacuna in the text. The missing part probably is not very extensive.

[18]A very small lacuna exists at this point in the text.

[19]This was an extraordinary penalty for such an offense.

[20]There is a lacuna of two and a half lines in the text of this poem.

[21]Grettir Asmundarson, outlawed at this time. The story of the relationship between Bjorn and Grettir is detailed more fully in _Grettis saga_.

[22]This probably is not a reference to the earlier poem by Thord on the occasion of Bjorn's lifting the new-born calf back into the stall, but a generic reference to a particular type of poem. The "cattle-poem" is also mentioned in the short saga of *Sneglu-Halli*, though it is not further defined there either.

[23]This verse is almost identical to verse 27 in *Eyrbyggja saga*.

[24]Both the name of Thord's Poem and Bjorn's nickname for Thordis are kennings for the sun. The poem apparently is a thinly veiled reference to Thordis.

[25]This is a blow to the back or buttocks, so-called because it would usually be delivered as the opponent turned or ran away.

[26]Probably Thord's men, the ones present at the meeting of Bjorn and Thord on Brenney Island.

SELECTED BIBLIOGRAPHY

This bibliography was prepared with the general reader in mind. It contains what English studies there are on the works in this collection with the exception of the shorter narratives and the *Bandamanna saga*, in which cases the entries are necessarily selective and were chosen to provide the most general coverage.

Andersson, Theodore M. *The Icelandic Family Saga*. Cambridge: Harvard Univ. Press, 1967. (contains material on all the sagas in this translation except *Króka Refs saga*)

Berger, Alan. "A Recognition Scene in *Valla Ljóts saga*." *Germanic Notes*, 8 (1977), 2-4.

________. "Lawyers in the Old Icelandic Family Sagas: Heroes, Villains, and Authors." *Saga Book of the Viking Society for Northern Research*, 20 (1978), 70-79. (on *Valla-Ljóts saga*)

Ciklamini, Marlene. "The Concept of Honor in *Valla-Ljóts Saga*." *Journal of English and Germanic Philosophy*, 65 (1966), 303-317.

________. "The Literary Perspective on Gisl Illugason's Quest for Blood Revenge." *Scandinavian Studies*, 38 (1966), 204-216.

Harris, Joseph. "Genre and Narrative Structure in Some *Islendinga þaettir*." *Scandinavian Studies*, 44 (1972), 1-27.

________. "Theme and Genre in Some *Islendinga þaettir*." *Scandinavian Studies*, 48 (1976), 1-28.

Hollander, Lee M. *The Skalds*. Ann Arbor: Univ. of Michigan Press, 1945. (Chapter 9, pp. 207-213 discusses *Sneglu-Halli þáttr*)

Palsson, Hermann. *The Confederates and Hen Thorir*. (The New Saga Library) Edinburgh: Southside, 1975. (a translation of the *Möðruvallabók* version of the *Bandamanna saga* and a general introduction)

Schach, Paul. *Icelandic Sagas*. Boston: Twayne Publishers, 1984. (contains material on all the sagas in this translation)

On the Skalds and their Art:

Frank, Roberta. *Old Norse Court Poetry*. *Islandica*, 42 Ithica: Cornell Univ. Press, 1978.

Hallberg, Peter. *Old Icelandic Poetry*. trans. Paul Schach and Sonja Lindgrenson. Lincoln: Univ. of Nebraska Press, 1975.

Hollander, Lee M. *The Skalds*. (see above)

Turville-Petre, E.O.G. *Skaldic Poetry*. Oxford: Clarendon Press, 1976.

www.ingramcontent.com/pod-product-compliance
Lightning Source LLC
Chambersburg PA
CBHW020618110726
47899CB00002B/555

9780819147042